A list of original
subscribers is printed
at the back
of this book

Penarth Beach in the days before the Pier was still a wild and windswept place. (PC)

PENARTH PIER

The Centenary Story 1894-1994

BY

PHIL CARRADICE

Published by
BARON
in association with
Vale of Glamorgan Borough Council
MCMXCIV

PUBLISHED BY BARON BIRCH FOR QUOTES LIMITED
AND PRODUCED BY KEY COMPOSITION,
SOUTH MIDLANDS LITHOPLATES, CHENEY & SONS
RAVENPRINT AND WBC BOOKBINDERS

ISBN 0 86023 511 4

CONTENTS

ACKNOWLEDGEMENTS

Many people have contributed greatly to the research and writing of this book, not least the residents of, and visitors to the town of Penarth. Without them the Pier would have gone many years ago.

However, particular mention must be made of the following: Miss Florence Evans, Mrs Florence Parry and Mr Malcolm Davies for their first-hand reminiscences of the Pier; Charles Carradice, Chartered Mechanical Engineer, for his detailed information concerning pleasure pier construction; Mrs Hazel Fearnley, wife of the late Tom Fearnley, for the loan of her husband's scrap book; Robert Galley, son of the late Stan Galley, for information and photographs of the Pier and of his father; Dr Don Anderson, Chris Collard and Nigel Coombes of the Paddle Steamer Preservation Society.

Thanks are also due to David Benger; George Best; Villis Kuksa of Penarth Framing Services; Rab Taylor of HM Coastguard; Brian Davies; Huw and Ron Bousie; Brian Stephens for the loan of his father's superb photographs of the *Port Royal Park* disaster; Colin Crayford of the Vale of Glamorgan Council; Richard O'Connell for the loan of his original paintings of Penarth.

Finally, I am grateful to the staff of Penarth Library, Glamorgan Record Office, the *Penarth Times* and *South Wales Echo*.

As ever, Trudy McNally deserves special praise — without her invaluable assistance this MS would have remained just another indecipherable MS!

PICTURE CREDITS

BD	Brian Davies	DA	Dr Don Anderson (of the Paddler Steamer Preservation Society)
BS	Brian Stephens		
CC	Chris Collard (of the Paddler Steamer Preservation Society)	GB	George Best
		PC	Phil Carradice
HB	Huw Bousie	R O'C	Richard O'Connell
WM&E	*Western Mail & Echo*	RG	Robert Galley
		VK	Villis Kuksa

INTRODUCTION

From the two pavilions at each end of the Pier strains of music came clear and precise on the night air. They were different — the New Pavilion echoed to the sound of Variety, the girls' voices high and shrill above the accompanying orchestra; from the old Bijou Pavilion at the seaward end of the Pier the lilting sounds of a foxtrot swept across the waves.

Piermaster Leonard smiled and shook his head. Young people today, he thought, didn't know what they liked. He was standing outside the New Pavilion, leaning easily on the railings, glad that yet another August Bank Holiday was almost over. Suddenly, he felt a hard elbow nudge into his ribs.

'Two excited kids', grunted his assistant, inclining his head down the pier. Leonard followed the man's gaze. Two youngsters were, indeed, charging along the decking, their hands waving and voices raised in alarm. 'Fire!' they screamed. 'The Pier's on fire!'

Instantly, Leonard and his assistant leapt for the fire hydrants and extinguishers but, at that moment, it seemed, the Pier burst into flames at their feet. Within two minutes a long stretch of the wooden decking, reaching from the old pavilion almost to the pier entrance, was a mass of spitting, snaking fire.

Later, with the benefit of hindsight, the *Western Mail* was able to comment that 'the pier must have been a glowing mass underneath before the first signs of fire were discovered'.

At the time, though, all that Leonard and his helpers could think about was the safety of the holiday-makers in the pavilions. It was the beginning of a long, hard night for the policemen, firemen and people of Penarth.

At the end of that night the Pier, Penarth's crowning glory, was a mass of twisted metal and rubble. To those who stared in dumb regret it seemed as if it had gone forever. And yet . . .

Penarth Pier suffered numerous setbacks in its brief but glorious career. There were many more to come in the days, months and years ahead but none of them were as dangerous or as potentially fatal as that dramatic fire in 1931. While it is probably appropriate to start this history of the Pier with reference to its moment of supreme danger, in order to fully understand the structure and what it meant to the people of Penarth, we must go back to the beginning. We must go back to a time when the idea of a pier — any pier — and a holiday resort were little more than faint glimmerings in the minds of those with power and influence in the community. Indeed, we must go back to a time when there was virtually no community at all.

Penarth Docks, the key to the town's prosperity; as a direct result of their opening, Penarth's future was secure and the development of the seafront made inevitable. (GB)

DOCK, BEACH AND FERRY

The first attempt to build a pier at Penarth occurred in the late 1870s and early 1880s. It was a short-lived project which ended in failure but by then the town had developed from its humble beginnings as a fishing village some three or four miles around the bay from Cardiff. Already it was a bustling, self-important community with ideas for its own development and, more important, the means of putting those ideas into practice.

In the first year of the nineteenth century the population of Penarth had been 72. By 1851 it had increased to only 273. And then came Penarth Docks. Two Acts of Parliament, in 1856 and 1857 respectively, granted permission for the Penarth Harbour and Railway Company to build docks at Penarth. The main impetus, perhaps naturally enough, was King Coal. Important and influential people like mine owner Crawshay Bailey, Robert Clive (or Clive of India as he was better known) and Baroness Windsor were all significant influences in the new company. The idea behind the new docks was to ease pressure on the grossly overburdened port of Cardiff. By 1854 the South Wales coalfield was producing 8,500,00 tons of coal each year and Cardiff Docks were rapidly reaching saturation point.

Consequently, the lower part of the Ely River was converted into a tidal dock and opened for trade in 1859. Work on Penarth Docks proper, on the other side of the Ely, had also begun and the facility was opened on 10 June 1865. The delay was partly due to faulty work by the original contractors but, once opened, Penarth Dock developed rapidly. In 1884 the complex had to be extended to keep pace with demand. Peak trade was achieved in 1885 with two and three quarter million tons of coal passing through the port. Although the docks then entered something of a decline,they remained for many years one of the major coal exporting ports in South Wales.

The town of Penarth grew quickly in the wake of its docks. A Coastguard Station was opened in 1864, standing high above the beach on the eastern edge of the town. A lifeboat station was also created, situated virtually on the beach, guarding the approach to Cardiff and Penarth Docks and the wide expanse of the Bristol Channel.

In 1851 there had been no named streets or roads, yet ten years later Ludlow Street, Salop Street, Glebe Street and four other roads were all named in the official census returns. The 1861 census gave a population of 1,923 — in ten years the population had increased sevenfold. By 1891 the figure had risen to a staggering 12,424!

The original houses were simple dwellings for labourers employed in building Penarth Docks. Most of these were imported and, as a result, came from places diverse as Cornwall, Gloucestershire and, in particular, Ireland. Wild and drunken behaviour was common, particularly on pay nights, and the new town quickly won a reputation as a rough place in which to live.

Soon, however, a different type of person began to appear in the fast developing community. Prosperous businessmen from Cardiff, many of them newly-rich industrialists connected with the docks or shipping trades, began to build houses for themselves in Penarth — away from the stench and clutter of Cardiff. These houses were elegant and substantial, in particular those in Marine Parade overlooking the beach and sea. Not surprisingly, these newcomers were far from happy with social conditions in their new town.

The problems did not lie just with Irish labourers. Residents could be dealt with — most of the wealthy property owners were JPs anyway, and could dish out summary justice as they chose. Visitors, however, presented a rather different problem. Penarth Beach had always been a great attraction and, as the town developed, each summer evening or weekend scores of people came from Cardiff and the surrounding areas to enjoy the delights of the shingle strand. Many travelled by road, a tollroad having linked Grangetown and Penarth since 1867. However, the vast majority came by water.

The Cardiff Steam Navigation Company was formed in 1856 to run ferries from Cardiff, *via* Penarth Docks, to Penarth Beach. The first boat, named *Conqueror,* was a tiny vessel but in 1865 a replacement, known as *Kate,* was ordered by the company. In due course another ferry, the screw-driven *La Belle Marie* was added. The company was bought out by Henry James Vellacott in 1883 and future developments included a new boat, *Iona,* and a second *Kate* (1893). Despite an increase in road traffic and the use of a public subway under the Ely River, the ferries continued to run every 20 minutes, providing a useful service until 1903.

The popularity of the ferry boats and of Penarth Beach led directly to the first attempted pier. The dates are unclear but somewhere around the early 1880s a London firm was contracted to build a pier and even went so far as to lay foundations and erect a few iron columns. The company then went into liquidation and all work was abandoned.

The proposed pier was sited close to the moveable landing stage for the ferry boats and it is quite possible that this pier was not so

10

much a pleasure pier as a functional structure to aid passengers disembarking from the *Kate* and *Iona*. The method employed to unload passengers was nothing if not original but it was not always safe or successful. The landing stage was mounted on four wheels and, when in the water, lay flat across the surface. It was pulled up the beach by a chain windlass when the tide was coming in but by a much more unusual method when it was on the ebb. Then the departing ferry would simply leave one of its mooring ropes attached to the landing stage and pull it further down the beach into a position suitable for the next boat. There is no definite proof for the surmise about the purpose of the pier but a more substantial landing arrangement would have helped the ferry boats immeasurably.

Britain has long had a fascination with seaside piers. It is important when considering Penarth Pier, its history and its future, to have some understanding, not only of how pleasure piers came into existence, but how they were actually constructed.

Simon Adamson, in his seminal work, *Seaside Piers*, has commented:

'Hypochondria was a popular pastime in the upper echelons of British society in 1800, and an industry had grown up to cater for the wealthy sufferers of real or immaginary illness. Harrogate, Boston Spa, Tunbridge Wells and, above all, Bath had prospered on the curative powers of their mineral springs.'

However, it was soon decided that seawater (smelling it, bathing in it, even drinking it!) was another potential aid for those with health troubles. Scarborough was the first important seaside watering place but by the early years of the nineteenth century Weymouth, Margate and Brighton had joined the list. Actually travelling to and from these places was something of a problem, however. Stage coaches and sail-powered coastal ships — the most popular methods — were notoriously slow and unreliable.

With the advent of steam passenger vessels after 1815 the journeys became much easier. Yet the real fun began when the boats arrived at their destinations. The difficulties encounterd in landing passengers had to be seen to be believed. Sometimes travellers were ferried ashore in leaking dinghies, their frock coats and heavy dresses invariably soaking wet at the end of the trip; at Ryde on the Isle of Wight day-trippers were actually given a piggyback on the shoulders of brawny sailors or porters. The sand or single was often strewn with luggage, the result of a careless unloading or lack of interest on the part of the ship's crew. Clearly something had to be done to enable passengers to disembark from the steamers in comfort and safety and, more important, at all states of the tide. The solution, of course, was to build piers.

Britain's first real pier at Ryde opened in 1814 and its example was quickly followed at other seaside towns. Brighton's famous Chain Pier was constructed between 1822 and 1823; then came Herne Bay, Walton-on-the-Naze, Southend and many, many more. Tolls were charged, both for passengers and for goods landed or taken on board.

It soon became clear that people were visiting the piers for reasons other than trade or travel. From the 1840s the word 'promenade' began to appear in the advertisements or prospectuses of pier companies. Casual strollers, it seemed, people who were willing to pay 1d or 2d to walk elegantly along the pier, were an excellent source of income for the pier companies.

The railway boom of the 1840s and '50s gave easy access to the seaside for all classes of British society. No longer were seaside resorts the preserve of a favoured few, as thousands of middle- and working-class trippers began to pour onto the beaches. They, like their wealthy counterparts, soon learned to enjoy strolling along the piers and promenades. The first real pleasure pier in the country was probably that built at Southport in 1859 but it was quickly followed by Worthing (1862) and Blackpool North Pier (1863).

The last twenty or thirty years of the nineteenth century saw almost 50 piers built around the British coast in what became virtually 'pier mania'. The 1871 Bank Holiday Act gave, albeit to a limited group of workers, the right to certain stated holidays and, as the century drew to a close, the concept of 'the weekend' became almost universally accepted. With increased intensity, trippers poured into holiday resorts, particularly over the August Bank Holiday, and pier companies were quick to realize the potential of their particular pieces of real estate. The piers soon became the centres of entertainment for seaside towns. No self-respecting resort could afford to be without one, each town striving to build a bigger and better example than its rivals. After all, the best pier invariably meant most visitors in the short summer season.

Why the pleasure piers should have had such a fascination for the British public is, in itself, an interesting question. To begin with there was the excitement which surrounded the pier — live entertainment in the form of minstrel troupes and dancers, ships and boats in the water below, a general sense of expectancy and fun. Then, of course, there was the fresh sea air and all of the beneficial effects it could provide. The beauty and elegance of fellow promenaders was always a great draw, particularly for the sauntering blades of the town or the maids and undercooks from the great houses on a rare day off. The pier itself was always an impressive sight, an architectural achievement which seemed to symbolise the might and power of Victorian Britain.

Above all, however, there was the stability of the pier. Elegant Victorian ladies and gentlemen could stroll along the decking or even sit in chairs at the end, contemplating the sea, sun and sky. To all intents and purposes they could have been at sea, but the one vital ingredient was missing. There was no sea sickness!

The piers were built of cast iron and greenheart timber. Cast iron was used for the legs and girder work because it was relatively cheap and did not warp. Iron always rusts initially, thus forming an iron oxide skin which then protects the metal from further corrosion. However, as a tension member it is not particularly good so, in order to accommodate the stresses of pleasure steamer berthing, greenheart timber was used at the pier heads — in other words for the landing stages at the ends of the piers where steamers actually tied up. The drawback to this system was that the wooden pier heads or landing stages would eventually rot away unless they were regularly maintained, a problem which beset Penarth Pier in the years immediately following the Great War.

The town of Penarth, then, though coming from an industrial base, was also conscious of its position as a seaside resort — Penarth had real delusions of grandeur.

By the early 1880s complaints were being made about 'the rabble from the hills' monopolising the beach. Some of these unwanted visitors had the temerity to dry their bathing dresses on wire lines along the strand; some of them even bathed naked in the sea! There were also complaints about the large number of donkeys on the beach and front — not for nothing was Penarth referred to then as 'Donkey Island'.

Therefore, in a definite attempt to upgrade the resort, Lord Windsor (the principal landowner in the district) conceived a plan which would exclude the rougher elements of the tourist trade and make Penarth a watering place the equal of Brighton, Worthing and the rest. The Windsor family seat was at St Fagans, some five miles inland from Penarth, but the noble Lord retained a passionate interest in his embryonic seaside resort. This interest was clearly not all philanthropy. The 'rabble' needed to be kept in their place. It was not by accident that the Victorians, at their divine worship, sang

'The rich man in his castle
The poor man at his gate,
God made them high and lowly
And ordered their estate'.

To disrupt the social order would be to alter the whole fabric of society. People were born into a particular station in life and that was where they should stay. Therefore, although the shop owners and business people of Penarth wanted trade, it was better to exclude the

13

workers and concentrate, instead, on those who could and should enjoy the facilities. Penarth, unlike Brighton and other towns on the south coast of England, did not expand from an upper class resort to take in working people. Rather, it was the other way round.

Robert Forrest, Lord Windsor's estate manager at St Fagans, was instrumental in getting things moving. Before 1880 there was no sea wall on the front facing the Bristol Channel. Two streams ran down the high, sloping cliffs, across the beach and into the water. The only buildings of note were the Kymin, Balcony Villa, Sea Cot and the lifeboat house. The beach itself was a pebble one but there was a flat sandy strip below the high-water mark. Being easterly facing it was not the most attractive of beaches but it did have superb views of Flat Holm, Steep Holm and the English coast.

To begin with, Forrest decreed, Windsor Gardens should be laid out. This elegant park, on a hill above the beach, was duly opened in 1880 and the public charged 1d for admittance. In 1885 the town Baths were built on the sea front, just to the north of the Windsor Gardens. Imposing in structure and style, the bath house had two swimming pools — a clear indicaton of what the Windsor Estate had in mind for the town. The Esplanade Hotel alongside the Baths, was opened in 1887.

The supreme achievement of Robert Forrest, however, was the Esplanade itself, built in 1883-4. Working in conjunction with Henry Snell, the architect for the Windsor Estate, and a freelance consultant called Barry, Forrest envisaged the Esplanade as a link with Marine Parade and Plymouth Road, thus forming a circular carriage drive around Penarth. Thirty-six feet wide, the road ran along the sea front in a north-south direction, providing an inviting and elegant promenade for strollers. At the southern end it climbed sharply up Cliff Hill, over 40,000 cubic yards of rubble having been cut out from the hillside in order to make the circuit complete.

Costings for the work are unclear, some reports saying £5,963, others giving figures in the region £10,000. Whatever the cost, the impetus (and much of the money) was provided by Lord Windsor. Its effect was startling. No longer did visitors have to pick their way over the stony beach; the Esplanade provided them with a modern, flat surface which would not damage their clothes or shoes. More important, it provided them with a stage where they could preen themselves and show off to their hearts' content.

There could be no doubt that Penarth had gone 'up-market'. Only one thing was now lacking — a promenade pier.

14

ABOVE: The entrance to Cardiff Docks, circa 1880; from here ferries ran, every 20 minutes, to Penarth seafront. The ferry boat *Iona* is against the jetty. (DA) BELOW: The ferry boat *Kate* unloads passengers on Penarth Beach; the landing stage lies flat along the surface of the water and, in the foreground, some of the work for the original Pier. (DA)

15

ABOVE: Penarth Station opened in February 1878 and, thereafter, hundreds of trip
poured into the town every summer's day. (GB) BELOW: The town of Penarth soon be
to grow wealthy, thanks to the tourist trade. This view shows the main thorough
Windsor Road, at the end of the nineteenth century. (GB)

16

PEERLESS PROSPECTS

On 29 December 1888 the *Western Mail* noted that
'The prospectus for the Penarth Promenade and Landing Pier Company Ltd, has just been issued. The share capital amounts to £35,000 in 7000 shares of £5 each, of which 2000 fully paid shares are to be allotted to the contractor in part payment for the works, leaving £25,000 to be subscribed by the public. Lord Windsor, the owner of the foreshore has granted the necessary licence for 99 years at the nominal rent of £25 per annum. It is expected that the pier will supply a long-felt want not only to the inhabitants of Penarth — the population of which has doubled in the last six years — but to the inhabitants of the surrounding district'.

Urged on by Robert Forrest and Lord Windsor, several Cardiff and Penarth businessmen had finally formed themselves into the Penarth Promenade and Landing Pier Company with the clear intention of providing the resort with the one facility it did not yet have — a pier. Prominent among them were the shipping magnate John Cory, Mr R. A. Bowring, Mr E. Hancock (of the Cardiff brewing firm) and Thomas Morel. Head office of the company was situated at 105 Bute Road in the docks area of Cardiff.

Drawing up plans and realizing the required capital took some time but by 1891 an engineer had been engaged and an application for an order to erect the Pier had been made to the County Council. The Penarth Promenade and Pier Order, 1892, was a substantial document which went into considerable detail about what could and could not be done.

The engineer for the project was Mr Herbert Francis Edwards of 21 Stanwell Road, Penarth. In the Order he was authorized to construct

'A promenade pier, jetty and landing place in the parish of Penarth . . . on the foreshore and bed of the sea adjoining that parish, commencing at a point two hundred and sixty feet or thereabouts measured from the northern end of the Esplanade in a southerly direction and sixty two feet or thereabouts from the northern end of a block of houses known as Balcony Villas, and extending seawards in an easterly direction six hundred and forty feet or therabouts and terminating in the sea with all proper works, sea walls, terraces, approaches, toll houses, toll gates, lifts, buoys, moorings, buildings and other conveniences connected therewith for the embarking and landing of passengers and goods, sewers and drains, and for other purposes. The pier shall be constructed in

17

cast-iron piles and columns, wrought-iron girders and timber deck open throughout.'

The contractors and engineer were allowed to deviate from the planned vertical height by up to five feet but, it was stressed, they must on no account 'extend the pier seawards more than six hundred and sixty feet from the high water mark'. The rationale behind this was quite simple. The channel into Cardiff Docks passed close by Penarth Head and a pier, or any construction which reached out too far into the stream would become a serious navigational hazard.

The Order also gave permission for the Company to erect on the Pier toll houses, seats, waiting rooms, concert rooms, aquaria and even, should they wish, a tramway. These buildings or services could then be hired out or sold, as the Pier Company desired. Once the Board of Trade gave its approval to the project, the Company would be able to charge in respect of boats docking and passengers, animals and goods being landed over the Pier. Not long afterwards such approval was granted, the following notes being written onto the architectural drawings of the Pier —

'In exercise of the powers vested in them . . . the Board of Trade approves of the pier which Mr H. F. Edwards proposes to construct at Penarth.'

The Pier Order document is a fascinating one, albeit couched in the singular language of officialdom. As well as setting out the charges and tolls for the Pier, it is quite specific in its instructions. For example, boats of 15 tons and under would be required to pay a charge of 4d if they wished to unload either passengers or cargo; up to 50 tons it would cost 6d and so on, up to a maximum toll of one shilling for all vessels over 150 tons. The Bristol Channel pleasure steamers would, obviously, come into the last category.

One interesting clause in the document concerned possible damage —

'Every person who willingly obstructs . . . setting out the lines of the works or who pulls up or removes any poles or stakes driven into the ground for the purpose of setting out the lines of the works, or defaces or destroys the works or any part thereof, shall for every offence be liable to a penalty not exceeding five pounds'.

Vandalism, it seems, was not a purely twentieth century phenomenon!

Work did not commence on the Pier for some time. Presumably the Company was experiencing difficulty in obtaining full financial backing. Shares costing £5 each were a heavy expenditure and only those with sufficient capital to spare could even consider investment. The shipowner Thomas Morel, for example, was happy to purchase fifty five £5 shares as well as three £100 debentures. Yet he was a wealthy man who owned other stocks and shares in investments such as the Barry Railway Company, in various collieries, in shipping lines and in banks. On his death in October 1903 the amount of share capital in his estate came to a staggering £267,794. Others were not so well placed. This did not mean that there was not interest in building a pier in Penarth. Indeed, quite the contrary.

Public opinion in the town ran strongly in favour of immediate constructon and there was even some talk about townspeople building a pier themselves. As late as 26 January 1894 the *Penarth Observer* was commenting

'We have long heard members of the Local Board grumble about the delay in building a pier, and some were anxious to take the matter over entirely, to show how quickly they could carry out the wishes of the public.'

In August and September 1893 a rumour began to circulate in the town that, rather than build a new pier, the Promenade and Landing Pier Company was proposing to buy a second-hand one from the town of Douglas in the Isle of Man. This pier had been built in 1869 and had already endured nearly 25 years of salt spray and battering from the elements. There was an outcry in Penarth. Nobody wanted a second-hand pier, not if they could have a brand new, gleaming example of their own.

The Editor of the *Penarth Observer* was not so sure. On Friday 22 September 1893 he wrote, under the headline 'The Proposed Pier at Penarth' that

'We are assured that the statement that an old pier from Douglas, in the Isle of Man has been purchased and is to be erected on Penarth Beach, is incorrect. We heartily wish it was not so. Any pier would be better than none, and no doubt the purchasers would be glad to sell it again at a reasonable profit. We do trust that another season will not be allowed to pass over without one of some sort being erected, but we understand that the one proposed will be altogether superior to the condemned one at Douglas'.

In the end the second-hand pier did not come to Penarth. Dismantled in 1895 it was bought by a North Wales businessman and re-erected at Rhos-on-Sea where it could rival the new pier at Colwyn Bay. Penarth, on the other hand, got its new pier.

After all the debate, all the infuriating delays and uncertainties, sufficient capital was finally made available. Work commenced on Penarth Pier in April 1894.

The contractors appointed for the job were James and Arthur Mayoh of Manchester. While the brothers cannot be viewed in the same light as the great pier designer Eugenius Birch (who built

19

Aberystwyth Pier in 1865), there is no doubt that they had considerable experience of pier construction and design. At Penarth they acted solely as contractors but they were also engineers in their own right. They had built piers at Great Yarmouth and Morecambe and, later, would construct another at the Mumbles, outside Swansea.

The new Pier quickly took shape. A working platform, or falsework as it was known, was built out from the Esplanade and from this, holes were bored in the beach and sea bed by huge augers. These were turned by teams of men pushing on bars similar to those of a hand capstan on a sailing ship. The majority of the labour was local to Penarth although, obviously, some specialists were brought in from outside.

The pier legs were cast in nearby foundries, brought out to the site on flat-bedded trailers and inserted into the bore holes. Once a group of them was in place they were cross-braced, tied and linked by beams to a previous set of columns. Slowly but surely the structure took shape, moving steadily forwards, out into the sea. Once the ironwork was completed the timber decking was laid and the builders moved on to finish the all-important landing stage at the seaward end of the pier.

The winter of 1894/95 was a cold one but the work continued steadily. By 5 February 1895 the *Western Mail* was able to report that

'The Penarth Promenade Pier is now an accomplished fact, and is available to the public. Although the pier is not yet used for excursion purposes residents and others may enjoy all the facilities at a small cost. Season tickets are now available at the office of the company, 105 Bute Road, or from Captain Evans, piermaster, at the pier.'

The design was relatively plain but the traceried balcony railings around the decking were intricate and ornate. Similarly, the two shops which stood at either side of the entrance were unusual in that they had tall, pointed, lead-covered roofs. A pair of rather elegant shelters broke the long line of the Pier, approximately halfway down its length. At 658 feet long and 25 feet wide it was not a particularly massive structure but the design had always been limited by the original Pier Order which forbade it reaching too far into the Channel. At the landing stage end the Pier doubled its width to 50 feet, to facilitate easier docking for boats, and stood approximately 50 feet above the seabed.

Penarth residents were delighted with their Pier and, after 5 February, flocked to experience the new attraction. Consequently, when the formal opening came two months later, a large number of local people had already walked out over the waves. The weather for the grand opening on 13 April was cold and wet but a large crowd gathered to witness the momentous event. The Pier was gaily decorated with bunting and the Cogan Brass Band was in attendance to play for the populace. The pleasure steamers *Bonnie Doon* and *Waverley* were the first vessels to call at the Pier and, as the former approached the landing stage, a salute was fired from the pier end. Amid loud cheers and a return salute from the paddlers, the first person to step ashore was Mr H. F. Edwards, the engineer who had designed both Pier and landing stage. There were no speeches, however, and soon the two paddlers had discharged and taken on passengers and set sail for Weston. Penarth Pier was formally open.

The rules surrounding use of the Pier were, initially, quite strict. No vessels were allowed to moor alongside, apart from the pleasure steamers, which would make routine calls to discharge and embark passengers, unless the Company gave explicit permission. The only exceptions were fishing boats forced to seek shelter in bad weather, and lifeboats. Toll charges were set as follows:

'For every passenger or other person landing on the pier from or embarking from it on board of any ship, vessel, packet or passage boat, for each time any sum not exceeding 4d.

For every person using the pier for the purpose of walking for exercise, pleasure, or any other purpose, except for embarking or disembarking, for each time any sum not exceeding 4d.

For every bath or sedan chair, including driver or carriers taken on the pier, for each time any sum not exceeding 4d.

For every perambulator, including driver, taken on the pier for each time any sum not exceeding 2d.

For every master of any vessel, boat, or wherry using the pier for the purpose of going to or returning from his own vessel, boat or wherry, an annual sum not exceeding £1.0.0.'

There were many other costs and charges. Trunks, boxes, portmanteaux, parcels and packages which were not actually carried by the passengers were charged 2d. If they were over 28lbs in weight the charge would be 4d.

The Directors of the Pier Company had grand designs for the future. They were not altruists but hard-headed businessmen with a clear eye for profit and further investment. The key to the success of their project lay in two areas — the promenaders, who would come, given the popularity of the Pier and Esplanade, and the pleasure boats which were to use the Pier as a landing stage.

Pleasure steamers had operated in the Bristol Channel for several years. The first genuine excursion steamer on the waterway had been the *Bonnie Doon*; the same *Bonnie Doon* which later made the inaugural docking at Penarth Pier. A Scottish-built paddler, she had been chartered by the Bristol Steam Yachting and Excursion Company in 1886 and was so successful that she was bought by a consortium of Bristol businessmen and sailed, again, the following year. This second season, however, she had competition.

Captain Alex Campbell and his paddle steamer *Waverley* were chartered by a rival concern, although Campbell did not skipper her himself as he did not hold a licence to operate in the Bristol Channel.

The *Waverley* was again so successful that Alex and his brother Peter decided to move their sphere of operations from the Clyde to Bristol. From 1888 the Campbells, no longer under charter but now working for themselves, began a series of pleasure cruises which, eventully, eclipsed all competition and made the name of their White Funnel paddlers synonymous with pleasure trips in the Bristol Channel.

In the early days, however, there was much competition. The first major opponents were Messrs Edwads, Robertson, a Cardiff-based firm which had acquired the *Bonnie Doon* and later added other vessels like the *Lorna Doone* and *Lady Gwendoline* to their fleet. The Campbells responded to this challenge by ordering a brand new vessel, the *Ravenswood* and later, the *Westward Ho*.

When Penarth Pier was opened for passenger traffic in April 1895 the battle for supremacy was at its height. With the *Bonnie Doon* the first ship to dock at the Pier, Edwards, Robertson seem to have stolen something of a march on the Campbell brothers but it was not to last. Later in the year the firm went out of business and sold their ships to John Gunn of Cardiff. Nevertheless, that first summer was a frantic one.

Campbells brought the brand new *Cambria* into service, while Edwards, Robertson had the *Lady Margaret*. The circumstances surrounding ownership of the *Lady Margaret* remain somewhat unclear, however. The firm was already in financial difficulties and it would appear that the bank was unwilling to loan them sufficient money to build the new ship. Therefore, the Lady Margaret Steamship Company was formed to build and run her. Many of the Directors of the new company were also Directors of the Pier Company and of Edwards, Robertson themselves.

This led to some confusion, with many people believing that the Pier Company actually owned the *Lady Margaret*. Not so. They did own several small vessels — rowing boats and the like — and even had a portion of the beach and sea wall reserved for tying up and beaching but the *Lady Margaret* belonged to a separate concern.

The Directors of the Pier Company had no reason to own or even consider owning pleasure steamers. They were making quite enough money as it was and steamship operation was always a risky business. They could afford to sit back, smiling and rubbing their hands in expectation. Their boat had, literally, come in!

ABOVE: Penarth Pier, in all its glory, is here on a summer's day at the turn of the nineteenth century. The paddler *Lady Margaret* is leaving the end of the Pier. (PC) BELOW: The Pier, viewed from the south side of the Esplanade, looks simple in design, even austere, but the intricate nature of the supporting piles can be clearly seen. (PC)

ABOVE: The *Bonnie Doon,* first vessel ever to call at the Pier, leaves Penarth c1898; (
Campbell's *Waverley,* the second vessel to call at the Pier, was a firm favourite with Pen
crowds. (DA) BELOW and OPPOSITE: Two artistic impressions of Penarth seafron
painter Richard O'Connell show a view of the north Esplanade, including the Esplan
Hotel, c1895 and look back along the length of the Pier, clearly showing the elegant she
half-way down the decking. (RO'C) BELOW: Penarth Pier is viewed here from Win
Gardens, c1905. (RO'C)

ABOVE: Shops flank the Pier entrance, and the turnstiles guard the way on in this early (1903) postcard. (PC) BELOW: This view of the northern part of Penarth Beach (later known as the Dardanelles) also shows the ferry landing stage pulled up above the tide line. (PC)

PROM, PIER & PAVILION

Almost from the beginning, Penarth Pier was an enormous success. And yet it was vastly different from almost all other seaside piers. There were no peep shows or honky tonk kiosks, no 'What the Butler Saw' machines to titillate young men who paraded up and down its six hundred feet length. There was, however, an indefinable flavour about a day on the Pier and beach. As Dan O'Neill, in an article in the *South Wales Echo* (20 July 1976), has said

'For generations of Cardiff school kids Penarth Pier was as close to an ocean liner as you could get. It made Penarth worth visiting — there wasn't much else for a youngster in that somewhat staid old seaside town.'

The lack of 'common amusements' was a deliberate ploy by the Directors of the Pier Company and by the wealthy residents of Penarth. Normally pleasure piers were a riot of good-natured fun. They had slot machines, strong men and circus freaks, fun fairs and loud music. Music hall stars like Dan Leno and Lilli Langtry regularly appeared at the their concert halls, while orchestras such as Mr Wolfe's German Band performed daily.

For many years pierrots were amazingly popular. Unique to pier entertainment were the divers, a strange breed of men who invariably called themselves 'Professor' Something or Other and leapt 30 or 50 feet, head first, into the sea for the amusement of the watching crowds. Sometimes tragedy occurred, as at Rhyl in 1887 when Tommy Burns, the world champion diver, was fêted and filled with so much ale before diving from the pier that he could hardly stand. He insisted on diving and was killed instantly.

Penarth had none of this. Such fripperies would not have been in keeping with the aims of Lord Windsor and Robert Forrest. Entertainments at Penarth consisted just of strolling on the Pier and Esplanade, of sitting in the sun on the seafront or in Windsor Gardens, or maybe taking a trip on one of the paddle steamers down to Weston or some other resort on the other side of the Channel.

Some limited and tasteful form of organised entertainment was provided, however, after a year or so. As early as December 1895, at the second AGM of the Pier Company, Directors were being questioned about the viability of providing a pavilion in which to hold concerts. By the summer of 1897, although the advent of a pavilion had to wait another 10 years, Messrs F. Darrell and Co of London had been engaged to produce a daily revue show on the Pier. The *Penarth Observer* (24 July 1897) commented

27

'Madame Albert E. Sibley, and Miss E. Vivian, are the lady vocalists and have given several charming ballads with rare effect. Mr Eisler Jones is the Comedian, this week and next, and his comical essays are encored nightly — "Poor Pa Paid", "The Giddy Little Gay Polka" etc etc. Mr F. Darrell, the manager, is singing some tenor ballads and they are much appreciated, more especially in "Polly and I" and "Red Rose and White". Altogether the entertainments are bright, refined and just what Penarth audiences appreciate."

The last sentence of this report is illuminating. Bright and refined — select in fact. How better to describe Penarth in the closing years of the nineteenth century? Such entertainments would probably have taken place in the open air or, at least, under a canvas awning. Either way they would have been easy prey to the elements. It was basic but it was an essential part of the Penarth scene.

Messrs Darrell and Co were extremely active on the Pier in the first few years of its existence. The *Penarth Observer* for 31 July 1897 commented that the week's entertainments had been exceptionally well patronized, despite inclement weather. The following week 'the one and only Odell' would appear, with several new songs including *The Burglar's Serenade*'. The paper also promised that, by public demand, the popular musical sketch *Crazed* would also be performed.

On 4 August Eisler Jones returned after a successful week at Walton-on-the-Naze, while Saturday 21 August marked the first appearance of a figure later to be well-known in the Penarth area. This was a young comedian and dancer by the name of Oscar Mills, the paper commenting that he 'sings some excellent songs, most of them being his own compositions. He dances well and his efforts to please are much appreciated.'

By the standards of the *Penarth Observer* this was no more than lukewarm praise. It is, perhaps, no surprise that, when Penarth next heard of Oscar Mills, it was not as a performer but as the first manager of the Pier's long awaited concert hall — the Bijou Pavilion.

There were, occasionally, wilder sides to entertainment in Penarth. The story has often been told of young boys who would climb out along the intricate girder work of the Pier, then suddenly appear over the guarding rail, frightening old ladies into fainting fits. Such tales may well be apocryphal but there is probably at least some element of truth about them.

No matter how much the upper classes of the town might deplore ordinary working people visiting the seafront, they could not actually stop them. By rail, road and ferry they continued to come.

Provided they paid their 2d admission charge the Pier was open to them as to anyone. The pages of the *Penarth Observer* in the 1890s and 1900s are full of complaints from local tradesmen about the tendency of working class people to prepare their own food on the beach. Such events, they stated, lowered the tone of the place. What they really meant, of course, is that it deprived them of trade!

A letter in the *Western Mail* in April 1898 complained bitterly about the lack of seats on the Pier and in the general area of the Esplanade: 'What few seats there are on or near the parade are generally occupied by "loafers" whose behaviour is not of the most refined description'. Clearly there was still a 'rough' element attracted to the town. As late as August 1900 the *Observer* was reporting that 'At the Penarth Police Court on Wednesday, a batch of Cardiff lads were charged with bathing opposite the Esplanade Hotel without being properly covered — John W. Norris, Robert Eddy, R. Youlden and Cyril Smith were fined 5 shillings each.'

This was just one of many such incidents reported in the paper, much to the chagrin of the upper echelons of Penarth society. At times they seemed almost to be waging war against those whose standards of behaviour did not match what they deemed appropriate.

One of the most common complaints in those early years, however, was about the pleasure steamers. On Saturday 2 May 1896, for example, the boat-keeper of Penarth Yacht Club, a man by the name of Searle, was working at the club moorings when the paddler *Cambria* came powering up to the Pier. The wash from her paddles capsized Searle's boat and tossed him into the water. Luckily he was able to swim ashore but, had he not been a strong swimmer, tragedy could have occurred.

P. and A. Campbell, when remonstrated with, expressed their regret but insisted that all of their Captains had been instructed to keep their speed down when approaching the Pier. They blamed the boatman for the problem, claiming that he failed to keep the bow of his boat to the paddler's wash.

However, just a few days later the cutter *Halogan*, belonging to Mr R. G. Laws of Penarth, was actually sunk by a steamer. Lying at anchor off Lavernock Point the wash of a passing paddler swamped the little boat and she went down rapidly.

Not long afterwards, on 10 August, the *Lady Margaret* — with Alex Campbell himself on the bridge — swamped a small rowing boat when she approached Penarth Pier at speed. Seven people were thrown into the water and the Inspector of Boats had to dive in to rescue them. The Clerk of Penarth Urban District Council wrote to Campbells, complaining.

29

The *Penarth Observer* for Friday 11 September 1896 reported Campbell's reply, saying that 'they much regretted the incident, and had again given the strictest orders on the subject, and suggested that all boatmen be requested to use a little more care in handling their boats'.

They probably had a point. The Council granted licences to boatmen and employed an Inspector to ensure that there were no maverick operators. At the end of the nineteenth century there were 14 such licence-holders operating off Penarth beach and they undoubtedly proved to be a nuisance for the speedy paddle steamers, particularly when there was a schedule to be kept. The heavy dresses of women passengers made rowing boats unwieldy at the best of times; with wash from the paddle wheels churning up around the Pier it is a wonder there were not more accidents.

However, the steamers must also bear some of the blame. Bigger and faster than rowing boats, common courtesy demanded that they take extreme care around busy stretches of water. Yet their skippers were mainly concerned with reaching their destinations as quickly as possible — beating the opposition boats and stealing their passengers was all part of the game.

Overloading was common. On 11 July 1900 Captain Ashford of the *Glen Rosa* was found guilty of carrying 797 passengers when his ship was licensed for only 541! Similarly, Captain M'Cloud of the paddler *Scotia* was once charged with overloading his vessel by 357 extra bodies. Small wonder, then, that the rowing boats off Penarth beach had problems.

Accidents and complaints continued for many years. On Tuesday 24 May 1898 a steamer approaching Penarth Pier almost sank the *Iona* when her wash lifted the tiny ferry boat out of the water and smashed her down onto a staging post of the landing stage. Luckily the post gave way or else the *Iona* would have capsized, with dozens of people on board. As it was, many were terrified by the accident and vociferous calls were made for a speed limit to be imposed around the pier head.

Complaints were also received about the short gangways between steamers and the Pier — fine for active and able-bodied seamen but not for middle-aged ladies and gentlemen or children. On Saturday 11 August 1900 the *Penarth Observer* reported Mr Westyr Evans as requesting that 'the Council support him in bringing pressure to bear upon the Board of Trade, to compel the provision of chain guards to the gangways used by passengers going on board the passenger steamers'.

Campbells were not the only firm to run pleasure steamers in the Bristol Channel. They may have seen off the challenge of Edwards,

Robertson, taking over several of their vessels from John Gunn in the last years of the nineteenth century, but there were always new companies with entrepreneurial ideas to challenge the supremacy of the White Funnel Fleet.

Serious competition, particularly at the western end of the Channel, came from Pocketts of Swansea who, for a while, seemed to have taken a firm hold of the Ilfracombe run. John Richards, again of Swansea, also competed in the same area between 1903 and 1907. The Barry Railway Company ran a fleet of paddlers and from 1905 — with the brand new *Gwalia* and *Devonia* — they ran the Campbells close. By 1911, however, their bubble had burst and in December the company sold its interests to P. & A. Campbell.

From the earliest days, the Pier was the scene of numerous suicide attempts. Just one sad story will suffice as an example. On Thursday 30 April 1901 a 50-year-old woman called Margaret Davies threw herself off the seaward end of the Pier. Nobody had suspected her intentions and the first most people knew was the sound of a loud splash in the water. One of the Coastguards and the park-keeper of Windsor Gardens ran for a boat but the woman was dead when they reached her. The *Penarth Observer* adopted a suitably chastening tone —

'It is to be hoped that a careful watch will be kept upon this spot for some time to come, lest her success — if it may be so called — should lead to a crop of imitators. Had this not been so local, we should have hesitated to publish for that reason'.

Despite all the complaints and problems there could be no doubt that the Pier was a considerable success. The Second Annual General Meeting of the Penarth Promenade and Landing Pier Company was held at the Esplanade Hotel on Saturday 14 December 1895. Thomas Morel was in the chair for a meeting which heard, from the statement of accounts presented, that there was a balance in hand of £613 13s 8d. The sum of £234 11s 2d was to be carried forward and an interim dividend of seven and half per cent paid. This was considered highly satisfactory as the Pier had only been open since February and boats had not begun to call until the summer.

One cautionary note was sounded when the meeting heard that P. & A. Campbell felt their company was, perhaps, not being treated totally fairly —

'The point was raised whether Messrs Campbell and Co could not be allowed to have an office on the pier, under the charge of a representative, as a rival company had. It was explained that Messrs Edwards, Robertson and Co, the rival company, who were in possession of an office there, did not rent from the pier company but from the owner of one of the shops. The general opinion then expressed was that if Messrs Campbell and Co applied for an office, the directors would be pleased to consider the matter.' (*Penarth Observer* 20 December 1895)

Considering the fact that the Pier Company Directors had interests in Edwards, Robertson and its subsidiary company, the point is a moot one.

Successful as the first year had been, it could not begin to compete with the glory of the next dozen or so years as the Victorian age gradually faded away to be replaced by the brief but golden idyll of Edwardian Britain. The Directors and shareholders of the Pier Company must have been content with their profits which quickly doubled and even trebled on the first year's returns. Promenaders in their thousands continued to visit while the paddle steamers of P. & A. Campbell ploughed up and down the Channel, full to the gunnels with eager, happy trippers.

One of the most popular trips from Penarth in 1906 was the long haul down Channel to stare at the wreck of HMS *Montagu*, the Duncan-class battleship which had run ashore on Lundy Island. All summer long paddlers circumnavigated the island as the waves and elements defeated salvage attempts. Slowly the *Montagu* was battered to pieces. Many photographs were taken, many postcards bought and many a Penarth public house echoed to the sad tale of the stranded vessel.

On 15 June 1910 Captain Robert Falcon Scott and members of his polar expedition sailed past the Pier on the *Terra Nova*. Towed by the aptly named *Falcon* and flanked by the paddlers *Devonia* and *Ravenswood*, the departure was watched by thousands of people on the headland and on the Pier. The party had spent seven days in Cardiff, being wined and dined by the civic authorities. Indeed, the city became the largest single financial supporter of the expedition. Scott, who left the ship when she was a little way down-Channel, was a poor organizer who invariably put duty and pride before practicalities. His attempt on the Pole was doomed almost before it began. He rejoined the ship in New Zealand and perished, along with four members of his polar assault team, after failing to reach the South Pole before the Norwegian Amundsen.

In 1907 a wooden pavilion, to be used as a concert hall, was built at the seaward end of the Pier. The people of Penarth had long called for such a convenience but the Pier Company was reluctant to risk the financial commitment, at least until they had achieved some return on their investments. There had always been a feeling on the Board that if Penarth residents wanted more modern facilities for entertainment, then they should subscribe for them — preferably by putting 'money up front'. The success of the Pier more or less forced the Directors' hand, however. If Penarth did not have a pavilion then holiday-makers would simply go elsewhere.

Known as the Penarth Pier Bijou Pavilion, the first manager was Oscar Mills, who had previously appeared as a comedian and dancer. He leased the pavilion from the Pier Company, thus ensuring an annual income. Provided he and his entertainers were then able to pull in the customers, most of the profit would be his.

Over the next few years Oscar Mills brought in dozens of acts and entertainers to perform for the holiday-makers. In the summer of 1910, for example, he presented his Royal Court Entertainers at 3.15 each afternoon and again at 7.30 each evening. The charge for this depended on where people sat. Prices ranged from one shilling to 6d and down to the cheaper seats at 3d. Afternon matinees cost only 6d and 3d, with the added incentive that 'Tea was provided, gratis, to all occupiers of the front seats at the afternoon performances'. (David Ings: *Penarth in Old Picture Postcards'* Vol 2).

On Sunday evenings Mills presented Grand Military Band and Orchestral Concerts. This was an unusual privilege for Penarth residents and visitors as Sundays were still regarded as sacrosanct and, if pleasure piers did provide any form of entertainment on the Sabbath, it was usually in the form of sacred concerts.

At the end of 1910 Oscar Mills relinquished the lease on the Bijou Pavilion. He was replaced by Alfred Newton who was to take charge of pier entertainments for the next twenty years. Newton, basically, followed the same routine as his predecessor. He offered evening and matinee concerts and brought in variety acts such as the Court Jesters and the Mad Hatters but varied the programme slightly with an occasional farce, musucal sketch or light play. Every so often he would bring in a few 'up-market' acts, such as Lila Fields' Celebrated Company of English Girls. These he featured in a Russian Ballet, giving particular prominence to Little Marjorie Fountain as the solo ballerina. Programmes tended to change weekly with favourite acts like Fred Rigg, Olly Oakley and Vivian Foster, the so-called 'Vicar of Mirth', being asked back time and time again.

The Pier now boasted shops and tea rooms, Salter's Pier Café and Tea Gardens being particularly popular. Salter's Café occupied the right-hand shop flanking the entrance and the tea garden stretched for thirty yards behind the Pier. Salter's did not have it all their own way, for alternative refreshment rooms were available in the Esplanade Hotel and in the block of shops and flats built on the Esplanade in 1904. Notable emporia in this block included The Cabin and Govier's Restaurant. On the north end of the beach — in the area later known as the Dardanelles (due to fortifications built there during the war) — were tented refreshment stalls, the best known being Mrs Norman's cockle stall. Visitors to Penarth, it seemed, were well catered for.

It was during this period, in the months immediately preceding the outbreak of World War One, that Penarth had its first change of Piermaster. Captain Evans retired and was replaced by Mr H. R. Leonard. The new Piermaster had previously served as a fisherman, as a sailor in the merchant marine and, for several years, had worked for Edwards, Robertson, the rivals to P. & A. Campbell. He joined Campbells in 1895 and served for nearly twenty years as Purser on the pleasure steamers. Clearly he was the ideal choice as Piermaster, a fact proved by the length of his service — 23 years.

In that hot and giddy period before August 1914 it was as if the golden days of summer would never end. There seemed to be an air of peace and calm, of contentment and ease, with everyone knowing his or her place. Of course, such sentiments are tinged with nostalgia and nobody can deny the deep under-currents of poverty and neglect which were papered over by the system. However, in a time when entertainment, and life in general, were simple and straightforward, it certainly seemed an idyllic age. Britain's strength on the sea and as an Imperial power were supreme and the owners of the pleasure piers basked in their own self-importance. Had they but known it, the world was about to change forever.

LEFT: The Pier may have been fairly simple in design but there was no mistak quality of the ornate railings. (PC) RIGHT: Here, from a Tuck's Oilette postcard, t Piermaster, Captain Evans, stands on the wooden decking. (GB)

ABOVE: In 1907 the Penarth Pier Bijou Pavilion was built on the end of the Pier. (GB) BELOW: Like a stranded whale the Pier stands high and dry at low water. (PC)

35

ABOVE: This view along the Pier clearly shows the entrance and, on the right, E. Salter's Pier Café and Gardens. The advertisement announces that 'Montague's Mountebanks' are appearing in the Bijou Pavilion at 3.15 and 8.00 pm. (GB) BELOW: In 1906 the battleship *Montagu* went ashore on Lundy Island. Many trips left Penarth Pier to view the stricken vessel. (PC)

PENARTH PIER

Lessee ... ALFRED W. NEWTON
Acting Manager ... A. R. PHERN

WEEK COMMENCING

˥ONDAY, AUGUST 21st

ily at 3.15 & 8   Doors open at 2.45 & 7.30

˥SPECIAL ENGAGEMENT of

˥ILA FIELD'S

Celebrated Company of

˥ENGLISH GIRLS

˥RUSSIAN^IN BALLET

˥o ACTS, and Third Edition, most Popular
Version of BRILLIANT REVUE

˥HERE WE ARE"

NEW SONGS

˥W DANCES   NEW DRESSES

NEW LONDON COMPANY

˥E: Two postcards advertise the appearance at the Bijou Pavilon of 'Lila Fields
˥h Girls' and 'Little Marjorie Fountain'. Such advertising cards were common in
˥dian Britain. (GB) BELOW: Captain Scott's *Terra Nova* sailed past the Pier in 1910.
˥are view shows her heading down-Channel, attended by the paddler *Ravenswood*.
(DA)

Penarth Pier and Penarth Head — aerial view. (GB)

CONFLICT TO COUNCIL

When war was declared in August 1914 there was little immediate impact on Penarth and its Pier. The weather that summer was glorious and the season was in full swing. There were more important things to do than to worry about Germany. And besides, the war would not last long. Home by Christmas, everyone said. Meanwhile, carry on as normal.

Soon, however, as the casualty lists from Mons and Ypres began to come in, as the Admiralty started to think seriously about defending the coast, things began to change.

It was the paddle steamers which went first. In September 1914 the *Devonia* and *Brighton Queen* were requisitioned by the Admiralty for conversion to minesweepers, followed in December by the *Cambria*, *Westward Ho*, *Glen Avon* and *Lady Ismay*. By July 1915 only the *Waverley* and *Glen Rosa* remained, but even their activities had been grossly curtailed, consisting mainly of short runs to nearby places like Weston. These last two White Funnel paddlers were duly called up for duty in May 1917.

After that, an ancient steamer, the *Duchess of Devonshire*, was chartered to make the regular ferry run between Cardiff and Weston. She may have occasionally called at Penarth Pier but this was a rare occurrence. Apart from anything else, with the German U-Boat menace at its height, not many people were prepared to even consider a Channel trip and the demand, therefore, was slight.

All of the paddle steamers gave valuable service during the war years, relentlessly sweeping for mines off places as diverse as Dover, Zeebrugge and the Dardanelles. Only the *Waverley* and *Glen Rosa* spent any significant period of their naval service in the Bristol Channel, sweeping the area between Swansea and Ilfracombe. Two of the ships, *Brighton Queen* and *Lady Ismay*, were sunk during the four year conflict.

Pier personnel also served in the armed forces. Piermaster Leonard joined the Royal Navy and served for the full four years, his ship, *Majestic*, being torpedoed in the Dardanelles. Like other members of the pier staff, his post was held for him so that he could return to his duties after the war.

Some time during the early part of the war, although the precise date remains unclear, Penarth Pier was requisitioned by the Army. Garrisoned by a detachment of Royal Engineers, a single searchlight was positioned on its seaward end, with the intention of providing illumination for the entry to Cardiff Docks. Two artillery pieces were stationed on the cliffs above the seafront, to work in conjunction with the searchlight, should the Docks be attacked by German surface raiders.

The idea behind mounting a searchlight on the Pier was simple. It is not possible for any searchlight to sweep from a high position such as the cliffs as, from such an angle, the light would produce only an arc. Therefore, the light needed to be low down to the water. Penarth Pier was an ideal location.

In 1916 the Officer in Charge of the REs was Lieutenant Christpher John Evans. He had been commissioned while serving at Penarth, having previously held the rank of Sergeant Major. His wife and young daughter, Florence, were with him during his posting and it is due to Florence's remarkable memory that we owe many of the details of Penarth Pier's part in the war effort.

The soldiers were billeted in the various shops along the Esplanade and on the rough ground between the Beach Shelter and Yacht Club. Lieutenant Evans had his office at the seaward end of the Pier, alongside the old Bijou Pavilion. The unit owned a black and white terrier called Tiger, which acted as a mascot. Miss Evans clearly remembers him running up and down the Pier, seemingly unconcerned by the sheer drop on either side. Indeed, this very lack of fear eventually led to Tiger's downfall.

In 1917 the REs moved onto Penarth Head, their searchlights being repositioned on specially constructed structures at the foot of the cliff. Tiger continued his playful ways. One day, unfortunately, he was too excitable, was unable to stop and went head first over the cliff. He was killed instantly.

Although the Army was nominally in charge of the Pier during those years there seems to have been some limited use by the public. The paddle steamers, of course, did not call — they were not working anyway. Yet some casual strollers were allowed onto the Pier and several of the shops remained open. Miss Evans remembers playing on a football machine which was situated on the Pier — the type which had miniature players fixed to long horizontal poles. Given a good, hard push the money which had been inserted for the game invariably fell back out.

The soldiers put on several shows for the Penarth public, using the Bijou Pavilion as their base. Miss Evans was employed to sell the programmes. On other occasions the soldiers themselves were entertained by amateur performers. All in all, it seemed an amicable enough arrangement.

After the end of hostilities, however, events took a rather unfriendly turn. The Pier had received something of a battering during its service career and, when it was de-commissioned and returned to the Pier Company, a considerable amount of work was needed.

After assessing the damage the Company put in a claim to the War Compensation Court for £7,228. Processing such a claim took some time. After all, Penarth Pier was not the only claimant. However, by early December 1922 it was clear that the claim had been rejected, the *Penarth News* for 7 December commenting 'Nobody can justify the absurd award of the War Compensation Court of £353 on the £7,228 claim of the Penarth Promenade and Landing Pier Company. It is an ill reward for war service, and wretchedly unjust to the people who have to bear the financial burden'.

The Pier Company had suggested that soldiers constantly marching up and down the Pier in their heavy army boots had seriously damaged their property. Lieutenant Evans was called as one of the chief witnesses and was able to prove that the soldiers *never*, at any time, wore their boots on the Pier. Indeed, army orders were quite explicit on the point — soldiers had to wear plimsolls, not boots, while moving around on the decking. Miss Evans clearly remembers the plimsolls being white with pink or red soles — hardly traditional army wear but obviously effective!

The majority of the damage was, in any case, located at the landing stage, not on the main body of the Pier. This was due to lack of maintenance rather than wilful or accidental damage. The jetty was made of greenheart timber and, like all wooden structures, needed constant, careful attention. With Piermaster Leonard and most of his assistants away at the war, the Pier Company had simply neglected to carry out basic repair work.

The issue was raised in Parliament, the local MP stressing that Penarth people felt the compensation award was an insult. Stanley Baldwin, Chancellor of the Exchequer, replied that he did not 'propose to suggest to the Tribunal that a rehearing of the case should take place'.

He did, nevertheless, advise that there was always the possibility of a claim to the Court of Appeal upon a point of law. It was, however, a hopeless case and the Pier Committee (and the people of Penarth) had no option but to accept the ruling.

By awarding such a small sum in compensation — the exact figure was £353 5s 11d, plus 40 guineas costs — the Compensation Court was acknowledging and paying for a limited amount of damage. This was reasonable and was only to be expected. The cost of reconstructing the landing stage, however, was a problem for the Pier Company, not the Government!

At the AGM of the Pier Company, held on 4 December 1922, the Chairman, John Cory MP, was clear that the award meant repairing or reconstructing the landing stage was now out of the question. If any of the work was to be carried out, Mr Cory said, the Company would be looking to the Penarth public to subscribe the necessary amount, either in shares or debentures.

The *Penarth Observer* summed up the feelings of the town when it commented 'Without doubt more would have had to be paid for commandeering a fried fish shop in a back street'.

As far as the people of Penarth were concerned, a dilapidated pier was largely unusable, except for some limited form of promenading, and was a deterrent to trade in the town. It was already being suggested that the Company might be interested in giving the Pier, or at least selling it on favourable terms, to the Penarth Council.

Certainly the Pier Company was now in a dire financial postion. For four years during the war they had been deprived of virtually all income and even after hostilities ceased the paddle steamers had more war work to do, sweeping the seas around Britain for stray mines. Therefore, it was the summer of 1919 before anything like normality returned to the Channel and, even then, Penarth Pier was in such poor repair that the steamers could not call.

Campbell's were already active, however, determined to dominate the pleasure steamer trade in the Bristol Channel. Penarth could only watch in anticipation as, in 1922, they took over Tucker's Yellow Funnel Fleet. This at last gave them unrivalled superiority in the Channel.

Alfred Newton had resumed his entertainments in what was now known as the Pier Pavilion. At Easter 1922 he was offering *Fancy Fair*, the production written and directed by Charles Heslop. This was to be followed, on 22 April, by Reginald Sellick's show *Folly*. People continued to come — 33,804 of them for the concerts alone in 1923. That same year a further 21,900 promenaded on the Pier. This was certainly far better than anyone could have imagined, considering the derelict state of the place, but the summer seasons 1921-1923 went on record as the worst ever known, both for the Pier and for the seafront generally.

No matter how many people came to walk on the Pier or listen to the concerts, they could not compensate for the lack of pleasure steamer traffic. Before the war an average of 200 people had embarked on or disembarked from the paddlers each day — somewhere in the region of 35,000 each summer season. With the landing stage out of action people now had to journey to Cardiff or Barry if they wished to use the boats, thus depriving Penarth of valuable tourist trade.

An exciting interlude occurred in June 1923 when a young Grangetown girl, Maggie Clarke, got into trouble while swimming alongside the Pier. A local lad went to her aid but did not have sufficient strength to bring her back to land. The *Penarth News*, takes up the story: 'amid all the excitement, Mr William Curtain of Cliff Street, Penarth, climbed the railings of the pier and, without divesting himself of a single article of clothing, he plunged from a height of 20 feet. It was a dramatic moment. A cheer rang out as he reached the girl and, after a terrific effort, he slowly made way for the shore with the girl firmly clasped in his arms'.

By 1923 the possibility of Penarth Urban District Council taking control of the Pier had become much more realistic. Even so, it was not an open and shut case. Many people subscribed to the view that it didn't matter much who owned the Pier; getting the landing stage open and the paddle steamers calling again was the most important thing.

Council meetings in February and March 1923 were full of debate about buying or not buying the Pier. A purchase figure had been given by the Company but, for the time being at least, it was kept private. Many councillors were opposed to placing on the rates what might well prove to be an expensive white elephant — a view which was often backed up on the letters page of the *Penarth News*. Mr George Tennant, for example, wrote in September 1923, stating 'If the present owners cannot see their way to put it in repair, it bodes ill for any outsiders. Where would the money to maintain it come from? Certainly not from visitors'.

Particularly vocal in his opposition was Mr G. L. Norris, who clearly believed that buying the Pier was an unnecessary extravagance. Others took the opposite view, remembering when Penarth was a lively place 'with bathing machines, donkeys and stalls on the beach'. Trippers used to come in their thousands but that was in the days before they transferred their loyalty to Barry Island. To reclaim its position of prominence, the pro-buying lobby trumpeted, the Pier must become town property and must be re-opened to the paddle steamers.

By early summer 1923 the decision had been made. After a personal appeal from John Cory, an important Penarth resident as well as MP for the town, it was agreed to reverse an earlier decision not to buy. The District Surveyor was instructed to cost repairs to the landing stage and the wheels of purchase were set in motion.

Proceedings dragged on. The summer of 1923 came and went and Penarth, the Cinderella of Welsh seaside resorts, suffered because the Pier remained derelict and closed to Campbell's steamers. On August Bank Holiday that year over 70,000 visited Barry Island. Penarth was totally overshadowed, not only by Barry, but also by St Mary's Well Bay, Swanbridge and Sully. Between them these three resorts received 19,000 trippers — an amazing total, considering how small and undeveloped they were. St Mary's Well Bay, alone, took a staggering 14,000. Penarth, on the other hand, had barely 10,000 visitors, six thousand coming on the Great Western Railway, the rest by car or 'bus.

Penarth's poor showing was not solely due to the unavailability of the Pier. The beach was in a bad state too, for two years earlier excavation work had begun on Beach Hill at the northern end of the Esplanade. The workmen were in the habit of dumping their rubbish on the beach, thereby creating a most unpleasant aspect for visiting trippers.

On 16 August 1923 the *Penarth News* ran with the following story 'Whether it was pleasant or otherwise, Penarth Councillors got a surprise last week when they heard that their offer of £5,000 for the pier had been accepted by the Pier Company'.

The estimated cost of repairing the landing stage was somewhere in the region of £20,000 but it was felt to be justifiable expenditure which would, in the long run, be likely to bring prosperity to the town. The following week the paper was claiming that the purchase of the Pier was 'the beginning of the development that is to witness the gradual growth of Penarth into a popular resort that will not be ashamed to hold up its head at the side of Barry Island . . . The other development will be at the Esplanade end of the pier, where it is proposed to put a concert hall, which can be used for various functions and meetings' at all periods of the year'.

It was hoped that when the new pavilion or concert hall was built, the old wooden one could be used as a shelter or even as a temperance bar. However, the transfer of ownership did not go particularly quickly. The Provisional Order for the transfer was received in July 1924, giving additional permission for the Council to widen the Pier at the landward end by approximatley 50 yards each way. The Order received Royal Assent on 1 August and in October the £5,000 purchase price was paid out to the old Pier Company. Penarth Pier was now formally owned by the town of Penarth.

ABOVE: This elegant block of shops and flats were built on the seafront in 1904. (BD) BELOW: Penarth Pier was unused during World War One — apart from the soldiers who commandeered it during the early years of the war. (PC)

ABOVE: Searchlights, originally based on the Pier, were eventually moved onto purpose-built platforms at the foot of Penarth Head. (GB) BELOW: During the war years there was a limited paddle steamer service in the Channel. This is the small *Duchess of Devonshire* which was chartered to maintain the Cardiff - Weston ferry service in 1918-19. (DA)

ABOVE: Campbells's steamer *Glen Avon* is still in war paint, on her return from naval service in 1919. (DA) BELOW: By contrast dozens of rowing boats line the beach and lie off the coastline in this later postcard view of the seafront. (PC)

Despite the fact that the Pier was virtually unusable after the war, entertainm continued. This programme for 1922 advertises *Fancy Fair*. (GB)

48

CAMPBELLS ARE COMING

P. & A. Campbell had originally been unhappy about the District Council buying the Pier. However, they soon withdrew their opposition and promised a restoration of pre-war services once the landing stage was repaired. The Council went on record as saying that they wanted the Pier ready for boats to call at Easter 1925 and even went so far as to grant Alfred Newton a new seven year lease on the pavilion. They had borrowed something in the region of £16,700 in order to complete the purchase and commence work on repairs, in addition to their own capital investment, and needed the place open for business as soon as possible.

By the end of October 1925 the plans for reconstruction of the landing stage had been drawn up, one interesting clause being the stipulation that only out-of-work Penarth men must be engaged to actually carry out the work. Rather than use wood, it was planned to rebuild the landing stage in reinforced concrete, a fairly revolutionary process in the 1920s.

Already there were doubts about the speed of the work. Despite the Council's claims, many people began to suspect that the landing stage would not be opened until well into the 1925 season. Regardless of the delays, the services of Mr Leonard were retained as Piermaster. It was a wise decision as he knew both the structure and the Pier as well as the routines involved in running such a place.

At a meeting in Bristol on 23 September 1924 at which both Campbells and the Council were represented, it was agreed that the new proposals for the landing stage should be modified. New mooring bollards were designed and the stage was widened by 10 feet. Leonard disagreed with the Campbells, however, when they suggested that a sandbank off the pier head should be dredged. He knew of no such bank, he said, and the matter was taken no further.

By Christmas 1924 repair work had still not commenced and now people began to despair of the landing stage being open for any part of the 1925 season. Considerable damage was sustained during heavy gales on Boxing Night. Huge seas pounded the seafront and for a while the Pier was awash. Several iron gratings, each weighing in the region of three hundredweight, fell onto the beach below. Planking, seats and drainpipes were also carried away.

In February 1925 the District Surveyor, Mr Edgar Evans, was forced to admit that, in light of slow progress, it was most unlikely that pleasure boats would be able to call that year. The concerts would continue and the shops would open as usual but the landing stage would probably not be operational.

With the coming of spring, however, things began to move. On 9 April 1925 the *Penarth News* commented 'The train track has now been laid to convey material to the Pier head and railings have been erected around the terminus. Although an awkward job, the lines have been run around the pavilion which is already booked for concerts'.

It was strange that the original Order of 1892 gave the Pier Company permission to erect a tramway on the pier. Over thirty years later just such a track was laid, albeit for more prosaic purposes than conveying passenger traffic. Quite what the promenaders and visitors to the pavilion entertainments made of the small steam-driven locomotive, which hauled concrete and steel to the landing stage, has not been recorded.

The first ferro-concrete pile was driven in at low water on the afternoon of Monday 11 May 1925. Lifted into place by crane, the pile was dropped into a six foot hole and cemented into place well before the tide came in to cover it. The second pile went in at low water on the following day.

All summer the contractors, Messrs Nott, Brodie of Bristol, worked on the Pier and landing stage. The Council had decided to re-deck large portions of the original Pier and, in addition, the landward end had to be widened in order to allow the new pavilion to be erected. It was a difficult summer. Alfred Newton had a poor season as the noise of repair work interfered with matinees and the audiences, as a consequence, had been poor. At a Council meeting in October it was decided, as compensation, to remit £25 of his rent.

Some Penarth residents, however, were determined to enjoy what they could of the summer. In June Piermaster Leonard reported that two youths had disregarded his warning and dived into the sea from the landing stage. He further reported that warning notices had been pulled down and that the danger of divers striking their heads on the new concrete piles (which were covered at high water) was repeatedly laughed at or ignored.

Plans for the New Pavilion were now drawn up. Designed to hold 600 people, there were also to be six shops, cloakrooms, a tea lounge and terrace and a promenade around each side of the pavilion. A novel suggestion was also put forward; the Esplanade should be extended around Penarth Head to the dock. A road and, perhaps, a railway line could then be laid directly to the seafront. Nothing came of the suggestion, however, and the idea was dropped.

Numerous complaints continued to be voiced about the length of time the pier repairs took. Councillor Fred Phillips stated, in December 1925, that 'the contract had been carried out in a most unbusinesslike way'. Eventually the agreement was extended, giving the contractors until the end of January 1926 to complete.

Despite heavy snow at Christmas 1925 and again in January 1926, work continued slowly but steadily. The *Penarth Times* of 4 February 1926 carried a curiously flamboyant report on progress. It shows the significance of the Pier and its importance to the people of Penarth.

'The work on the Pier is going on by leaps and bounds, and dozens of hammers are tapping out a reassuring message that the boats will be coming at Easter. The landing stage is now taking very definite form, and barring accidents and extremely bad weather, should be completed before long. The re-decking is now well in hand and half the Pier is up ready for the new beams etc, to be laid. Underneath the Pier, suspended like spiders, and walking upon iron struts that any self respecting chicken would think twice about roosting on, modern Blondins from Cogan are playing around as if a forty or fifty foot drop into the tide on a winter's day was nothing. Their endurance and fortitude is really amazing as they chip, chip, chip away with little hammers, removing the rust and old paint that has been hardened for years by the weather. One fellow, whilst warbling "Yes, sir, that's my baby," moves across from one narrow strut to another with only his pal's outstretched hand between him and below . . . with a coolness and a sangfroid that Harold Lloyd would envy. The weather is bitterly cold and the wind makes it difficult to hang on to the iron work but they are there, day after day'.

The landing stage was finally completed later in February, with the first pleasure steamer scheduled for Easter Wednesday, 7 April. It was to be a special trip to Weston and was to be 'invitations only'. On the appointed day the old favourite *Glen Avon* eased in to the landing stage and Councillor C. P. Deverall cut the ribbon to formally declare the Pier open once more. The dignitaries then sailed away across the Channel as crowds cheered the departing paddler.

Between April and Whitsun a limited steamer service was provided by Campbells who did not regard the season as beginning until May. From Whit Monday onwards, however, it was a full service, for the first time since the high summer of 1914. Work still continued on the main Pier but this did not prevent Alfred Newton opening his season at the Pavilion with the comedy play *Artistry*. One of the leading actors, Fred Rigg, had been a regular performer at the Pier in pre-war days. On the same programme Newton presented a concert party, the Marvellos, a mental mystery act. The first performance took place at 3.00 pm on Easter Monday.

The District Council issued new charges, announcing them in the *Penarth Times* for 8 April —

'Persons Promenading 1d
Passengers Landing or Embarking 2d
Return Ticket, Landing or Embarking . 5d
Single Ticket, Landing or Embarking .. 3d.'

It was a good summer, despite a curious problem which arose in August. A strong and unpleasant smell began to ooze off the beach. The contractors, still working on the pier, were blamed as they constantly pulled seaweed out of their pumps and allowed it to rot on the beach. A long-winded debate ensued. Some people acknowledged the smell, others said that, as the tide came in twice each day, the seaweed was thoroughly washed and that therefore no smell existed. In the end the Council sprayed disinfectant on the weed and obliterated the odour.

Sea angling soon became popular, as the structure provided an ideal base. The Pier and Esplanade Committee of the District Council decided to ban fishing with hand lines, however, insisting that only rods could be used. Moreover, anglers were permitted to use only the south side of the Pier. It was to be another seven years before the Penarth Sea Angling Club was formed but the upsurge of interest in fishing seems to date from around that time.

Despite the fact that Mr Newton had planned a full season of entertainment — booking people like radio star Vivian Foster, a musical group called the Gamblers and the popular P.P.P. Company, he was forced to curtail his shows at the end of August. The noise and inconvenience caused by the widening of the Pier and by the commencement of work on the new pavilion were just too much. In addition, the economic state of the country did not auger well for an extended season. Quite simply, there was not much money around.

The next few years were a combination of hot summers and happy visitors but with increasing difficulties as the pavilion gradually took shape. The income from pier tolls had increased sharply since the District Council took control at the end of 1924. For the first year the income had only been £11 1s 10d — hardly surprising considering the state of the Pier and the work taking place. In 1926 it rose to £238 7s 5d, and in 1927 it mushroomed to £756 2s 6d, mainly due to a full season with Campbell's White Funnel Fleet. In 1928, as construction work on the new pavilion began to bite into the visitors, the toll income dropped to £659 6s 10d — still an excellent figure. In addition to the pier tolls there were rents for shops and the old pavilion. In 1928 alone this amounted to £195.

End of season festivities now always took place at Penarth Pier — a large party which traditionally accompanied the last sailing of the summer. Fireworks, fancy dress and streamers were the regular order of the day in those years between the wars. It was a tradition, however, which survived World War Two, lasting until the final demise of the paddlers in the 1960s.

Despite the General Strike and problems of unemployment, the Pier had proved a positive acquisition for the Penarth Urban District Council. When the New Pavilion finally opened they could confidently look forward to even better times.

On 9 May 1929 the *Penarth Times* was finally able to announce 'The New Pavilion, which Penarth has been waiting for so long, will be opened on Saturday evening next, Mr Newton having engaged as his initial attraction the 'Lido Follies', a new and unusual type of song and dance act. The opening night promises to be one of the biggest social events ever held in Penarth'.

The New Pavilion was a unique structure, being constructed entirely from ferro-concrete and covering an area of 4,000 square feet. It was a massive building, if not beautiful then at least startlingly impressive. It was given a cupola roof and several dormer single windows. There was a wide entrance and vestibule, with the main hall on the ground floor measuring 95 feet by 42 feet 6 inches. A large balcony and seating accommodation for 600 people faced a stage measuring 44 by 21 feet.

Despite its imposing appearance, however, the New Pavilion could not hope to compete with the elegance of the old shops and tea rooms with their delicately pointed roofs. These, unfortunately, were demolished when the Pier was widened. The concrete shops which replaced them were functional but that was all. Some small link with the past was retained as the old gate to the Pier was kept and used to guard a side entrance.

The constructors for the pavilion were Messrs E. J. Smith of Cardiff, although the widening of the Pier, which preceded building, had been carried out by Macdonalds from Abergavenny. All the labourers came from Penarth, as the Council required. Some controversy was aroused by the tendering arrangements for the internal lighting of the pavilion, local firms feeling they had been excluded from the competition. In the end the lighting was installed by Messrs Metro-Vick Supplies, with Julians of Cardiff putting in the stage equipment.

The official opening of the New Pavilion took place at 5.00 pm on 18 May 1929, the ceremony performed by Mrs A. Pertwee, Chairman of the District Council. Following the ceremony she was presented with a small gold key by E. J. Smith, the contractor. The National Anthem was sung, as well as two solos by Madame Venn, and there were several speeches, notably from Sam Thomas, Chairman, of the Pier Committee. The cermony concluded with Miss Doris Pawley singing *Land of Hope and Glory* and *Rock of Ages*, before the Welsh National Anthem brought proceedings to a close.

The *Western Mail* commented, fulsomely, that 'today Penarth can boast of having a sea front equal to that of any of its rivals'.

The paper was undoubtedly correct. Since 1921, when work began on improving Beach Hill, the Esplanade had been widened (making a pedestrian promenade over 20 feet in width), the Pier had been totally renovated, a new pavilion had been built and the elegant Italian Gardens (1926) opened. It all gave a new, distinctly superior feel to the sea front.

The opening concert in the New Pavilion took place at 8.00 pm on 18 May, a few hours after the official ceremony. It was, reportedly, 'a veritable riot of colour', with serious items interspersed with light-hearted material. Prior to the concert there had been a *Prologue* which was written by Alfred Newton and recited by Miss Barbara Weight. It was hardly great poetry but it is worth repeating in full, simply to give a glimpse of the atmosphere in Penarth on that day:

'Good people all, we meet tonight to launch a scheme ambitious,
Created by your Councillors, who thought the time propitious
To try their best to boom our town and add to its attraction.
They hope this New Pavilion here will meet with satisfaction.,
A scheme of which this was a part, in '25 was started;
The Pier, then almost derelict, its usefulness departed,
Came into your possession, and your Council, though oft slated,
Decided then to reconstruct, and many plans debated.
At first the landing stage was built, a necessary measure,
Which gave access to Channel boats, and added to your pleasure.
The work on this was slow but sure; Father Neptune oft objected
But the following year the job was done, and an April day selected
When Councillor Deverall cut the tape — a pleasant little function
Your Council took a Channel trip — I think there was a luncheon.
Then after this a project bold, which you have since enjoyed,
The widening of your Esplanade, gave work to unemployed.
This work, when finished, was the cause of much felicitation,
The noble Earl of Plymouth came to give congratulation.
Mr Stanley Smith, your Councillor (hard work must be his hobby)
Then laid a stone to celebrate, which now is in the lobby.
And when the pier was well restored with bases firm and steady,
This hall was then decided on, as everything seemed ready.
A most respected Councillor, a JP I might mention,
Was Chairman of Committee, and devoted much attention
To find how best to raise the wind, as schemes like this cost money.
Financial needs were soon o'ercome, then everything looked sunny,
An engineer most highly (Highly) prized helped your Surveyor in
planning;

54

An architect 'ere Summerset (Somerset) was found to do the
planning.
They got a Smith to do the job — I trust my puns won't bore you —
This building, which is quite unique, the first one of its kind,
Is raised in ferro-concrete, not a single brick you'll find.
There's no need now to tramp the Pier when to the show you're
getting,
And should the weather prove unkind, you need not get a wetting.
And now that trade is looking up, and coal is selling brightly,
If short of tons, come to the Pier; you'll get a New Ton nightly.
And now, kind friends, it rests with you to make success quite
certain.
My Prologue's o'er, the Follies wait — Let's now ring up the curtain!'

The rather heavy handed puns refer to notable people connected
with the New Pavilion — the architect, engineer, Newton himself
and so on.

Penarth Urban District Council had paid out approximately
£7,000 for the repair of the landing stage, nearly £4,000 on the
repairs to the Pier and £6,000 for the widening and reinforcing of
the shore end. The New Pavilion cost somewhere in the region of
£9,000 to build — altogether a cost of £26,000 for work on the Pier
alone. When alterations to the Esplanade and Beach Hill were
added, the full cost of the extensive repairs and restoration came to
over £30,000.

Now the Council and, indeed, the whole town felt that they could
look to the future with hope and relief.

Without its Pier, Penarth lost out heavily to tiny resorts like ABOVE: St Mary's Wel
and BELOW: Lavernock in the immediate post-war years. (GB)

56

The paddler *Glen Avon* was the first vessel to call at the Pier once the
Council had repaired the landing stage. (CC)

ABOVE: The Italian Gardens were built on the Esplanade, after the war.
(PC) BELOW: The New Pavilion was built at the seaward end of the Pier
in 1929 — gone is the elegance of the old Victorian structure, yet nobody
could deny its imposing appearance. (PC)

ABOVE: The New Pavilion, seen from the Pier, has an almost eastern feel. (GB) BELOW: The Esplanade Hotel — here in a 1930s advertising card — was built in 1887 and damaged by fire in 1977. (BD)

A Punch & Judy show on Penarth Beach. (GB)

DANCING IN THE FLAMES

Even before the New Pavilion opened there had been considerable debate about the future of the old one. A leader in the *Penarth Times* for 18 April 1929 stated 'At present it is dirty and untidy, and something should be done to alter the present condition of things before the season sets in'.

One of the earliest suggestions was that it should become a shelter and general entertainments hall, perhaps a temperance bar where trippers could buy a glass of milk and a bun. In June 1929 Councillor Slater was suggesting that it could be converted into a skating rink or dance hall. The opposite opinion was eloquently put by somebody signing themselves 'Frequenter of the Beach' in a letter to the *Penarth Times* at the end of April 1929 — 'Surely the greatest argument for building a New Pavilion was that the present one was not only dilapidated and rotten,, but was not worth repairing! It is simply a hideous, temporary erection which never possessed any architectural beauty or dignity, and gives a most unfortunate impression of Penarth to all who pass or approach our town by the sea'.

Throughout the summer of 1929 the old Pavilion lay unused, becoming more and more unsightly by the day. Events on the Pier went on as normal. In late July the National Orchestra of Wales performed in the New Pavilion, a concert which was enjoyed by some but felt by many more to be 'too highbrow'. Falkman and his Orchestra, the next attraction, proved to be much more popular.

The Town Carnival was held on Wednesday 18 September, when Mr G. Pugsley organised sideshows, quoits, shove-ha'penny and other attractions on the Pier. The event was excellently attended with trippers arriving by train, 'bus and Campbell's steamers for the carnival.

In October 1929 plans for conversion of the old Pavilion into a Dance Hall and Shelter were submitted by the Surveyor to the Council. For an estimated cost of £1,000 it was proposed to re-lay the floor, erect a new roof and build a shelter alongside the landing stage. This, it was felt, would be another good investment.

The New Pavilion — or the Pier Pavilion as it was now called — was rented out, once Newton's season had finished, to private groups and individuals. Between 24 February and 1 March 1930, for example, it was hired to the Operatic Society for £25. Earlier on, when the Junior Imps performed there at the end of December, the virtually arctic temperatures provoked a storm of criticism and a demand for improved heating. There were other complaints about the poor paintwork on the building and the fact that the stage facilities were too small.

The Council fielded these complaints but otherwise did little. They simply did not have the money. For the same reason the original plan for the old Bijou Pavilion was shelved as being too expensive. A sum of £100 was approved, basically to give the place a 'lick of paint', and that was about all that could be expected.

In November 1929 a memorial clock was presented to the town and mounted outside the Pier Pavilion. Donated by Mrs Esther Harries, in memory of her late husband, Hyman, and her son, Solly, who had been killed in the war, it was unveiled on Wednesday 20 November. A memorial tablet, in both Hebrew and English, was also erected.

For the 1930 season Alfred Newton planned performances by professional companies, interspersed by amateur shows — the Penarth Operatic Society with their production of *Merrie England*, for example. Loudspeakers played records during the day, not just in the Pavilion but also along the Pier and on the Esplanade. The general mood was one of contentment and ease.

The old Pavilion opened for business once more — run, incidentally, by the Council — with the Regatta Dance on 21 June. Over 200 dancers filled the building and dozens more were unable to gain admission, so popular was the event.

On 16 October 1930 a benefit concert was held for Mr Newton, who was retiring as lessee of the Pavilion. He had spent 20 years running the entertainments at Penarth Peir and had stuck by both the Pier Company and the Council through some fairly desperate times. Often, rather than have his artistes go away empty-handed, he had given the Company far more than he had ever taken at the door. At the benefit concert everyone — artists, performers, musicians and stage hands — gave their services free.

In November the Pier was the scene of an interesting tussle between a fisherman and his prey. An angler found he had a heavy bite and struggled for nearly fifteen minutes to land his catch. When he got the fish up onto the Pier it was discovered that he had hooked a thresher shark! Over three feet in length, the catch caused considerable interest among other fishermen and onlookers.

Perhaps the most devastating incident in the history of the Pier took place on the evening of Monday 3 August 1931 when a large portion of the structure was destroyed by fire. Writing under the headline 'Penarth Pier and Dance Hall Burnt Down', the *Western Mail* of the following day began its report in graphic style — 'Writing under the glare of the still blazing structure, with the smell of smoke heavy in the nostrils, it is not easy to get back to the beginning of things about an hour and a half ago.'

It has never been made clear how the fire began. All that is known is that it started in the old Pavilion, in all probability when a casually discarded cigarette fell through the dance floor and ignited accumulated rubbish below. After smouldering away for some time the flames erupted with startling suddenness at about 9.00 pm.

Soon the whole Pier was a raging blaze and panic set in. The 200 people dancing in the old Pavilion rushed for safety. Halfway down the Pier they met a crowd from the Pier Pavilion and Esplanade who, having seen the flames, were charging the other way to see if they could help. Disaster was imminent.

However, members of the theatre orchestra and policemen who had dashed to the scene were able to link arms and push the crowd back to the promenade. They left a wide lane at the side of the Pier and along this the majority of dancers were able to escape.

Twenty to thirty people were unable to get out before the flames cut off their retreat. They took refuge on the concrete landing stage, where their plight was noticed by Inspector MacDonald of the local police. He immediately contacted the Yacht Club and seven boats rushed to take off the trapped dancers. Two of these boats capsized in the heavy seas, however, and the occupants were thrown into the water. They were eventually rescued by other craft but for a long while it was not known if any of them had drowned.

The local fire brigade, under Captain A. E. Mayne and Second Officer George Fluck, had by now arrived on the scene. Together with the pier staff and police they fought an heroic battle against the flames. Gradually, however, they were pushed back towards the shore. Just after 10.00 pm the old Pavilion colapsed in a shower of flames and sparks. The two shelters on the centre of the Pier followed in quick succession.

By 10.30 there was an inferno of flames stretching for almost 100 yards along the Pier. At approximately 11.00 pm, however, the flames were suddenly and dramatically cut off from land when the central portion of the Pier collapsed into the sea. By now nearly 500 people were watching the disaster from the Esplanade, beach and Penarth Head; the flames were clearly visible several miles away down-Channel. The collapse was something of a minor miracle as, with nowhere to go, the fire eventually burned itself out at about midnight.

Inspector MacDonald later commented 'I have seen hundreds of fires but I have never seen one spread like this. When I got there there was just a cloud of smoke. Before we could reach the pavilion there was a sea of flame. It was exactly as though the blaze ran along a train of gunpowder'.

Mr Leonard Zanoni, musical director of the Moonbeams Company, then playing in the Pier Pavilion, had been standing at the stage door when he saw 50 to 60 people dash along the Pier. Realizing that the structure was on fire, he ran back into the Pavilion and told the orchestra to play *I'm Happy When I'm Hiking*. He then got everyone to march, to this tune, out onto the Esplanade. There was no panic. Then, with the rest of the Moonbeams — who had dumped their props in the middle of the road — he formed a chain to stop people coming back onto the Pier.

Heroic deeds were numerous, not least by the Moonbeams, who helped fight the blaze, still dressed in costume and in grease paint. One pierman recounted, later, how he had come across the prostrate body of a girl who had been overcome by smoke. He carried her to safety through the flames. Other pier hands had to struggle with drunken men who failed to see the danger and had to be dragged to the shore.

Patrick Cavanagh, a young motor mechanic from Plassey Street, was dancing with Miss Margorie Langford when the cry of 'Fire!' was raised. Thinking his girlfriend was with him he rushed outside and had nearly reached the Esplanade before he realized she was missing. Immediately, he went back to search for her. However, she had already left by another exit and Cavanagh, in his desperate efforts to find her, was severely burned.

Mrs Nellie Diggins was working in the kitchen of the old Pavilion when the alarm was given. She was unable to escape and found herself trapped by the rapidly spreading flames. She managed to attract the attention of a man outside, Mr Jim Jenkins, by knocking at the window with a bottle of lemonade. Mr Jenkins helped her through the window and, together, they made their way to the landing stage where they were later rescued by a boatman called Murphy.

Several members of the band from the old Pavilion lost their instruments and equipment in the fire. One of them, a drummer by the name of Mander, estimated his lost drums to have cost something in the region of £40, a considerable amount in those days. The flames, he said, had seemed suddenly to leap through the floor. Most of the day's takings on the Pier — a large sum as, being August Bank Holiday, there had been many visitors — was lost in the blaze, as well as dozens of coats, bags, hats and other property belonging to the dancers.

As the fire brigade began coiling their hoses, another fire erupted at the Llandough Saw Mills and soon they were away up Beach Hill to extinguish their second blaze of that night. For the majority of people, however, once the fire died there was nothing to do but head home.

As it turned out, nobody was killed but there were several injuries. The Pier itself was probably the worst casualty. When dawn came up the following day there emerged a scene of complete and utter desolation. Metal girders had been twisted like hairpins while charred wood was strewn for miles along the coast. At low tide many of the dancers returned to search the beach for their property — but everything had been reduced to ash.

For the children of Penarth, however, there was a positive side to the disaster. Mrs Florence Parry (née Lovegrove) watched the fire from the Promenade, in the company of a young friend, like many other people of the town. The following morning she remembers searching the beach for coppers which had fallen from the buckled and melted slot machines on the pier. She and many other youngsters had a successful haul.

The immediate problem for the Council was how to keep the steamers coming. Initial fears of a total disaster soon proved ungrounded; the blackened, 'beached whale' appearance of the Pier was somewhat deceptive. No serious structural damage had been done, at least none that could not be repaired. The concrete landing stage was virtually intact and, apart from the central portion of the Pier — which had burned away and collapsed — it was felt that the structure was usable. It would certainly be no use for promenading but as a means of getting people onto the steamers only minor work had to be done. The Council promised to provide a gangway over the damaged portion and were as good as their word. On 21 August the *Penarth Times* was able to report 'Although the Pier gangway was opened on Friday evening — a day before it was expected — sixty four people made use of it, either for embarking or landing from steamers. The first steamer to call was the 'Glen Avon' . . . three more calls were made during the evening and the following day a large crowd pased through the turnstiles. Several notices drew attention to the 'No Smoking' rule which was strictly enforced'.

Entertainments at the Pier Pavilion continued, unchecked, for the rest of the summer. The big advantage was that it was on the landward end of the Pier, unlike the old pavilion. Therefore, the repair work, which soon got under way, did not greatly affect performances. Some visitors were undoubtedly put off by the bruised and blackened Pier but the vital factor was that they were still able to embark on the all-important paddle steamers.

By the following year things were back to normal, all repairs completed. The first pleasure steamers of the 1932 season left Penarth for Weston at 10.40 am on 24 March and soon it was business as usual. An agreement was reached that passengers on Campbell's steamers would no longer have to pay a pier toll. While the charge was incorporated in the money the White Funnel Fleet paid to berth the psychological factor was important — trippers felt they were getting something for nothing. The only people who did not greet the news with enthusiasm were the Pier season-ticket holders. They would receive no concessions and, if they chose to take a trip on the paddlers, would effectively pay twice.

The total cost of re-building was £3,157 but, significantly, the Old Pavilion was not replaced. Many Penarth residents thought it was a mistake. One letter to the *Penarth Times* believed it was 'a huge blunder. It certainly was an attraction and the Pier receipts will, I am sure, suffer considerably in consequence'.

Nevertheless, the Council stuck to their decision. They judged the day of the Bijou Pavilion over. From now on formal pier entertainments, if they were to exist at all, would have to take place in the new Pier Pavilion.

Holiday-makers disembark from the Campbells' paddler in the late '20s. Judging by the coats and mackintoshes it has been a wet day. (PC)

An advertisement from the *Penarth Times* announces *Modern Follies* at the
New Pier Pavilion. (PC)

ABOVE: Penarth seafront; the Pier Pavilion dominates the scene in 1929. (PC) BELOW: The old Bijou Pavilion, here at the end of its life, was used as a dance hall once the New Pavilion opened. (PC)

The Penarth Pier Fire.

THE BLAZING PIER.

The newspaper of 6 August 1931 headlines the destruction of Pier and
Pavilion (PC)

ABOVE: Despite the fire, it was soon 'business as usual', on Penarth seafront. (GB) BELOW: Penarth Regatta, seen from the Pier, was a regular event on the seafront for many years. (PC)

WAR STOPS PLAY

Throughout its history Penarth Pier has greeted and seen many famous people. After Captain Scott there were many others.

Gracie Fields once promenaded when she stayed locally, although there is no record of her ever singing in either of the two pavilions. Lord Baldwin — or Stanley Baldwin, Prime Minister, as he then was — called at the landing stage while taking a trip on a Campbell's steamer. A large crowd gathered to cheer him and Baldwin acknowledged them gracefully.

In the late 1920s Sir Alan Cobham, the famous aviator, was supposed to land a seaplane alongside the Pier. The event was advertised in the local and national press and nearly 1,000 people paid their toll to gain admission to the Pier. Then came the news that Cobham was landing in Cardiff Bay instead. A mad dash ensued for the exit, nearly carrying away the pier gates.

So many famous ships have passed that it is almost impossible to record them all. From giant battleships of the Home and Channel Fleet to elegant liners, from wooden walls like the *Havannah* (one of the vessels which escorted Napoleon into exile and later became a nautical training school at Cardiff) to the Royal Yacht *Britannia*, they came. And Penarth Pier stood solidly to watch their passing.

The largest crowd ever assembled on the Pier was a staggering 4,000, who came for a fête and carnival in 1926. Such a figure seems unbelievable now, with safety regulations which would prohibit even a quarter of that number. Yet it must be remembered that the paddle steamers themselves regularly carried loads of 600-plus and, provided there was room to breathe, nobody was going to complain, particularly not the Council, who were happily counting the tolls.

By the early 1930s, however, public tastes were changing. People no longer promenaded; if they used the Pier now, it was usually for a stroll in the sun, to embark on the pleasure steamers or to play on one of the many slot machines which began to make their appearance. The days of revues and variety shows were also drawing to a close. Talking pictures had already made their appearance and the Pier Pavilion saw a gradual falling away of audiences. This was, to some extent, expected. There were already two cinemas in the Penarth area — the Regal and the Windsor Kinema.

Therefore, it was no great surprise when Messrs Cooper and Wright of Newport took over the lease of the Pavilion and announced they were going to turn it into a cinema. On 3 March 1932 the *Penarth Times* announced 'Patrons of the Pier Pavilion may or may not have regrets that in future concert parties will not provide their entertainment, for at the moment workmen are busily engaged installing the latest sound system for the provision of talking pictures at a cost of about £3,000. A company has been formed, known as The Lyceum, Penarth Ltd.'

The grand opening was fixed for Easter Monday (prices 7d, 1s or 1s 6d) with the feature films *Bad Girl* and *Two Crowded Hours*. The first programme was a great success with large crowds queuing to gain admission, even though the two films were of such mind-boggling mediocrity that they have since vanished without trace. For a long while there was standing room only. Performances on the following day were equally well attended.

By April 1932 the cinema directors had negotiated with a local 'bus company (Harfoot) to run a service every 15 minutes from Cornerswell Gardens to the town centre and, thence, to the pier. Formal opening of the cinema, with speeches from local councillors, took place on 18 April. On 14 May the cinema opened an outdoor café alongside the Pavilion, to be run on 'continental lines, with the exception, of course, that wines cannot be served. From Saturday next morning coffee can be taken in charming surroundings from comfortable "Blue Train" chairs in orange, green and blue. High class coffee, mineral waters and cakes, and a special equipment for Eldorado Ice Cream has been installed'.

The Pavilion Cinema closed in October 1932, despite initial promises that it would stay open all year round, with a view to making a few minor alterations and installing a new heating system. It was supposed to be closed for a few weeks but it was Easter 1933 before it opened again.

Attendances during early summer 1933 were not good but, despite requests from the directors, the Council was not prepared to either wait for, or waive, the rent. The company was faced with a heavy deficit. However, it came as a major shock when, on Saturday 24 June, the management dismissed the staff and closed the establishment.

The summer was exceptionally hot and Campbell's steamers were well employed with trips to places as diverse as Clovelly, Tenby, Minehead, Ilfracombe, Lynmouth and Lundy Island. The Pier Pavilion remained firmly closed however, a fact which was much lamented in the local press. The following description of the scene on Penarth Pier seems to sum up the holiday atmosphere of that summer — an atmosphere made, perhaps, all the more poignant, by the fact that Adolf Hitler had already come to power in Germany and the strains of Nazi martial music were already beginning to be heard throughout Europe: 'Boats were coming and going, and people were hustling and trying to get through the altogether inadequate turnstiles . . . The piermen wore only the clothes that decency demanded, and were extremely helpful to passengers with luggage. The destination of each boat was loudly and persistently called, and there was no occasion for anyone to get bothered or flustered. The piermen were at hand to help here and there, and put you and your luggage on the right ship for sailing the seas in a prompt and courteous manner, and this despite the torrid temperature and the crowds'.

It is sometimes easy to forget that the steamers were not only used for pleasure trips. People going on holiday to Weston-Super-Mare or Porthcawl, to Ilfracombe or Tenby, would use the paddlers to reach their destinations, just as easily as they would by train or motor car. It all added to the hustle and bustle of the pleasure piers.

By the following summer Penarth Pier Pavilion was being used as a theatre once again and then, in July 1934, came the news that the Council had an offer from a group of local businessmen to turn it into a dance hall. It was originally intended to call the new emporium The Dansart but, by September, the name Marina was adopted. A new floor was laid and the Marina Ballroom duly opened for business in October 1934. Hundreds danced to the music of Wilfred Muchawek and his band. In the interval there was a cabaret provided by Madame Grayce Goldwin, with Jack Corsi on the piano accordion. A regular programme of dances followed that first night, afternoon sessions lasting from 4.00 until 6.00, evenings from 7.00 to 11.00 pm. A sun parlour was also created at the pier end of the Pavilion to provide an added attraction for dancers.

As the 1930s wore on, a regular pattern was established for Penarth summers. Holiday-makers came in their thousands and the pleasure steamers continued to enjoy great success. Loudspeakers again provided a constant background of music. Public opinion was divided about this background noise, some believing it charming, others expressing the view that it was an assault on the ears.

There were walks along the cliff-tops, sea-bathing, cafés, golf courses and the swimming baths; each evening the Marina offered dancing and a welcoming atmosphere. An advertisement for the ballroom, dating from Thursday 9 April 1936, gives a good impression of what was on offer over that Easter weekend —

'Good Friday   open pm and evening
                    for teas, refreshments and music
Saturday   Tea Dance, 4 - 6.00 pm
                    Evening Dress Dance, 8.00 till midnight
Easter Sunday   Open pm and evening
                    for teas, refreshments and music
Easter Monday   Tea Dance, 4 - 6.00 pm
                    Special Long Night Dance, 8.00 - 1.00 am
                    2s 6d exclusive (dress optional)'

The same advertisement announced that the music was to be provided by the Marina Band, directed by Bobby Bruce. Formed and recruited in London, this was billed as their first appearance in Wales.

By 1936 the manager of the Marina was Mr J. S. Blundell, who had been one of the moving forces behind the conversion of the Pavilion into a dance hall in 1934. He did much to popularise the centre, running dances throughout the year. These were invariably well-attended, the New Year's Eve Dance for 1935/36, for example, catering for nearly 400 revellers.

On Saturday 7 July 1934 a dramatic incident occurred on the Pier when an unknown woman climbed onto the railings and threw herself into the sea. As the tide was on the turn, she fell almost 30 feet into water which still had a ten-foot depth. Four bathers, who were swimming nearby, immediately went to the woman's aid and pulled her out, uninjured.

The idea of swimming in the sea around Penarth Pier seems, now, to be an appalling prospect. Yet in those days, before pollution — or, perhaps, knoweldge of pollution — outlawed the habit, the seafront was a bather's paradise. Many people used the landing stage as a diving base and then swam back to the shore. Sailing and rowing boats constantly moving back and forth along the coast simply added to the scene.

In the autumn of 1937 Piermaster H. R. Leonard retired after 23 years in post. The position was advertised on 5 October, offering a salary of £200 per annum. Candidates had to hold a Board of Trade Sea Going Certificate for Master Mariner or for Chief Mate. There was an upper age limit of 45 years, unless the candidate had served in HM Forces. The Pier Committee Minutes for 20 December record that nine candidates were shortlisted and that Mr J. Kinnersley was appointed.

Kinnersley took up his appointment in the New Year but on 21 June 1938 the Pier and Esplanade Committee of the Council was told he was unhappy about his accommodation. The Piermaster's house stood on the edge of Windsor Gardens (a similar property on the other side of the gardens was occupied by the Park Keeper) and, while undoubtedly pretty, it was also inadequate. It was, complained Kinnersley, noisy and it was also impossible to stand up in one bedroom. It was estimated it would cost in the region of £350 to make the place halfway decent.

The complaints attracted little sympathy, the general feeling being that £350 was a great deal of money to spend when there were many other parts of the town, and many other Council properties, in worse condition. One Councillor, Captain W. A. Pritchard, commented 'This man accepted the job with this house. If he doesn't like the house he can easily resign. There are plenty of people in Penarth who would take this house with the job'.

In the end some minor alterations were made and Kinnersley stayed. There was also a minor disagreement with the Penarth and Cardiff Sea Angling Club during the year. Founded in 1933, with their inaugural meeting on Friday 20 October at the Gwalia Café on the Esplanade, the Club had always worked in close harmony with pier officials. But now Leonard had gone and the relationship with Kinnersley had yet to grow.

Consequently, the *Penarth Times* was soon reporting that people who frequented the Pier were complaining about pieces of bleeding fish and bait left lying on the decking. Windows in the Marina had also been broken by weights, when anglers cast their lines. Kinnersley supported Mr Blundell, the Managing Director of the Marina, in the complaints. The Club secretary acknowledged the problems but denied his members were responsible. No satisfactory conclusion was reached and the matter soon died.

In February 1939 Piermaster Kinnersley was commended by the Board of Trade. He had given valuable assistance when the sailing vessel *Matilda* got into difficulties on 22 October the previous year. Three men were rescued.

The Minutes of the Pier and Esplanade Committee for 22 May 1939 seem blissfully unaware of the approaching conflict which was then only four months away. They report that new records were to be ordered (to the value of £5) so that different music could be played over the Pier and Esplanade speakers. The British Automatic Company had just agreed to supply one dozen new slot machines. Other purchases included 50 deckchairs for the Pier and 50 for the Esplanade. A deckchair attendant was to be employed to look after them.

When war finally came, its effect was immediate. The *Penarth Times* for 7 September 1939 commented 'Owing to the outbreak of war, Messrs P and A Campbell's White Funnel Fleet steamer trips have been completely cancelled, with the exception of a daily service between Cardiff and Weston. There will be no sailings from Penarth Pier'.

The following week, even the Cardiff - Weston services was cancelled. The Bristol Channel paddlers were immediately called up for service, only the old *Ravenswood* remaining in 'civvies' (until 1940). Employed again as minesweepers, the story of their war is well told in Nigel Coombes' *Passenger Steamers of the Bristol Channel*. Suffice to say that the ships performed with heroism and spirit, particularly at Dunkirk, where three of them, *Devonia*, *Brighton Queen* and *Brighton Belle* were lost. Later in the war the *Waverley* and *Glen Avon* were also sunk.

Penarth Pier was closed to the public almost immediately but it is apparent that, bit by bit, limited public use returned. The decision to restrict public use is understandable. The threat of air raids was great — indeed, the town became a target for enemy bombers on many occasions, particularly between 1940 and the summer of 1941. Seven people were killed in the town during these raids and many more were injured.

The Pier Committee Minutes for 22 January 1940 record that Piermaster J. A. Kinnersley RNR, was given permission to join the Navy. He served throughout the war, rising to the rank of Commander. Kinnersley left on 14 February and Mr A. C. Vincent took charge in his absence.

The Minutes of 18 March 1940 state that all deckchairs (presumably those on the Esplanade, not the Pier) were to be vacated each day at sunset. This was to aid blackout regulations. Deckchairs seem to have been an important issue as, on 17 February 1941, the Town Surveyor reported he had loaned six for a Fire Watching Party. Despite reservations about possible loss of their property, the Council agreed.

At the start of the war two six-inch guns were mounted on the cliff above Penarth. Manned by the Glamorgan Heavy Artillery Regiment, these were descendants of the guns placed there during World War One. Early in the war, however, the guns were taken away and a small battery of three inch artillery pieces was put into Cardiff to defend the Docks. The searchlight platforms at the foot of Penarth Head, within easy sight and reach of Penarth Pier, provided the base for an 'illuminated area'. The searchlights and guns, both in Cardiff and out on Flat Hoilm, came under 570 Coast Regiment.

The Marina was still in use, with the occasional dance held for servicemen and locals. A Boxing Tournament also took place in the hall on 16 December 1940. As the war progressed and fears of a German invasion died away, some of the more stringent rules about use of the Pier were relaxed. After January 1941, for example, old age pensioners were allowed to fish off the Pier, provided they could offer evidence of age and pay the 1d toll. By May 1943 the Council was ordering that deckchairs should again be placed on the decking during daylight hours.

After hostilities ceased some repairs were obviously necessary. As with any war economy, for six years Britain's main thrust had been into the war effort and maintenance of structures like the Pier had been neglected. By 18 February 1946 the Minutes of the Pier Committee recorded considerable work already completed on the timber decking but a great deal of wood still needed. On 28

February, the surveyor notified the Council of the seriousness of the problem, pointing out that there were only a few firms in Britain that could do the work. Repairs were needed, not just to the decking, but also to the concrete columns of the landing stage and main beams of the Pier. He estimated that the labour costs alone would be about £850.

There were also staffing difficulties. In May 1946 one of the pier hands was suspended because of his conduct and told to remain off work for a week. The Pier Committee, meeting on 6 May 1946, resolved to recruit and pay for three deckhands, in addition to a Piermaster. The hands would receive £4 16s 0d for a 47-hour week, plus one shilling per head for any overtime worked.

The Easter holiday saw huge crowds on the Pier but there was an almost total lack of deckchairs and many complaints were made. Similarly, on August Bank Holiday later that year, vast crowds thronged the seafront but the Council did nothing in the way of entertainment. The *Penarth Times* was vociferous in its condemnation.

The Marina officially re-opened on 2 May 1946. Local MP Jim Callaghan had hoped to be present but was detained elsewhere. Local Councillors were there, however, and everyone was impressed by the quality of the redecoration.

On 16 June J. A. Kinnersley resigned as Piermaster, moving to Skegness, where he took control of all entertainment and activities on the foreshore. Quite what the Council felt about his departure — having kept his post open throughout the war years — is not recorded. He was replaced by one of the most famous characters in Penarth folklore, Stan Galley, who was to spend 24 years as Piermaster.

The White Funnel steamers returned to their peacetime duties in 1946, initially with the paddlers *Ravenswood, Glen Usk* and *Britannia*. The service was, necessarily, a restricted one as Weston Pier was in need of considerable repair and the one at Minehead had been totally destroyed. Penarth Urban District Council was proud of the fact that Penarth Pier, on the other hand, was up and running.

Campbells had definite plans for the future. Two new ships, the *Bristol Queen* (1946) and *Cardiff Queen* (1947) soon joined their fleet. Magnificent vessels, they were the latest word in paddle-steamer design and it was hoped that they would take pleasure cruising on the Bristol Channel into new realms of success. In reality, however, the two ships presided over a tragic decline.

ABOVE: Penarth Head is viewed here from the Cardiff side of the Ely River. (PC) BELOW: The Piermaster's house stood at the edge of Windsor Gardens — pretty but not practicable, as Piermaster Kinnersley soon found out. (RG)

78

PENARTH PAVILION, CINEMA

PHONE: 372 PENARTH.

Directors:
SIDNEY COOPER (Chairman).
H. J. PETTY.
MRS. R. COOPER.
F. NORMAN-WRIGHT (Managing Director).

Secretary:
J. McDONALD.

London Office:
17, BERNERS STREET,
LONDON, W.1.
Telephone: Museum 1927.

PAVILION,
PENARTH.

March 24th, 1932.

To the Residents of and Visitors to Penarth.

The Pier Pavilion will be opéned on Easter Monday at 2-30 p.m. as a First Class Cinema, with the best and last word in efficient Talking apparatus.

The Theatre has been equipped with additional heating and lighting effects.

Two hours and fifty minutes entertainment will be provided in each performance, and a continuous performance will be played until 10-15 p.m. each day.

No longer will it be necessary for the residents of Penarth to travel many miles to see the latest film or possess their souls in patience for many months waiting for it. The films to be shown at the Pier Pavilion will be placed before you at the earliest date.

The Theatre will be conducted on the highest possible lines and the experience of my Directors and myself will be concentrated on presenting a programme equal to any Leading London Cinema.

The first programme, commencing Easter Monday, will include the latest Universal News Reel and a great Fox production " BAD GIRL," featuring James Dunne and Sally Eilers; also the greatest Comedy Drama of the day, " TWO CROWDED HOURS," followed by a Comedy Film and suitable Musical Interlude. On Thursday, March 31st, two great Paramount Films will be shown: Marlene Dietrich in " DISHONOURED," and " UP POPS THE DEVIL."

SIDNEY COOPER, Junr.,
Manager.

The following Great Artistes will be screened at the Pier Pavilion in their latest productions in the immediate future:—

RUTH CHATTERTON.	MARLENE DIETRICH.	JANET GAYNOR.	ELISSA LANDI.
RICHARD ARLEN.	VICTOR McLAGLEN.	CHARLES FARRELL.	JACK BUCHANAN.
SALLY O'NEIL.			WARNER BAXTER.

In 1932 Penarth Pavilion Cinema opened and this advert appeared in the *Penarth Times* the week before that. (PC)

ABOVE: This dignified view of the Esplanade gives a good indication of the traffic on the seafront in the 1930s. It also shows the public rooms of the Esplanade Hotel. (BD) BELOW: Penarth Pier at low water. (HB)

HIT THE DECK

In August 1946 there was an interesting debate in the Letters Column of the *Penarth Times*. On 22 August, Mrs L. S. Reid wrote, complaining — 'What do you think of my 2 year old son being told by the Piermaster on Sunday to stop running around as the people came to the pier to rest? I haven't seen any notice requiring "Quiet Please", and thought that as long as no damage was done, the pier was free for all kiddies to enjoy themselves. What sort of place is this?'.

The following week, somebody signing themselves GEA put the opposite side of the affair — 'The action of the Piermaster . . . is to be applauded. The Pier has, I believe, been generally regarded as a place where one may spend a few pleasant hours and it would be a pity if it would be allowed to develop into anything even remotely resembling a playground'.

The letter went on to applaud Piermaster Galley's actions. If children wished to run around, said the writer, they should be taken to the beach or cliff-tops. The Pier was the place for a quiet snooze, not rowdy high spirits!

However, its peace and solemnity were rudely and abruptly broken the following year when, on the evening of Friday 2 May 1947, the Canadian steamer *Port Royal Park* was driven dramatically into its north side. For a while it seemed as if the structure had been damaged beyond repair.

The *Port Royal Park* had sailed earlier in the evening from Newport. She had a pilot on board and was bound for Cardiff Docks, where she was to take on a cargo and then depart for the Persian Gulf. At 7,131 tons she was a large vessel and her master, Captain Yool, was an experienced seaman. However, a gale was blowing and the strong tides of the Channel took her beyond the entrance to Cardiff Docks. Before pilot, captain and crew realized the danger, Penarth Pier loomed up ahead of them in the gloom.

Three men were on the Pier, two anglers and Coastguard William Jones, who was on duty. As the *Port Royal Park* was driven against the Cardiff side, they took to their heels and ran for the safety of the Esplanade.

The regular Friday night dance was being held in the Marina, with dancers blissfully unaware of the impending danger. The thump as the ship hit the Pier, however, brought reality harshly home. In the end the vessel's bows finished up a few feet away from the ballroom — disaster had been averted but not by much!

81

Mr J. A. Brown, superintendent of Penarth Baths, was one of the first to take action. Alerted to the danger he saw a gas pipe on the Pier fracture under the impact. Racing across the road he immediately cut off the gas supply, thus preventing a major explosion. He also warned dancers and helped them to the safety of the Esplanade.

Once the immediate danger was over, the Pier staff and local police were able to take stock. The *Port Royal Park* lay broadside on to the north side of the Pier, her giant superstructure dwarfing the buckled planking. Luckily the tide had just turned and was now going out. This meant that the ship lay relatively calmly against the Pier — further grinding or pounding on a rising tide could well have meant that the whole structure would collapse.

News of the incident spread throughout the town and soon hundreds of spectators were lining the Esplanade. The following morning over 1,000 cars were parked on Penarth seafront, their owners anxious to see what damage had been inflicted.

Even at this early stage it was obvious the Pier had sustained serious damage. The wooden decking was shattered and buckled, almost for its entire length, while the northern shelter had been smashed into the centre of the walkway. By far the most serious damage, however, was to the cast-iron supporting columns. Over 70 were fractured and pushed out of alignment. At first sight the injury seemed terminal.

Something had to be done — and quickly — as the tide would soon turn again. The risk of further damage was real. The *Penarth Times* for 8 May commented 'After the crash the captain was assisted to the Pier by Police Sergeant D. Rees and then travelled to Cardiff to make arrangements for tugs to tow the vessel'.

Most of that night Captain Yool was busy in Cardiff, command of the ship left in the hands of Chief Officer Frank Martin. By early morning, however, the skipper was back on board. At about 5.30 am three tugs duly arrived and stood by. The *Port Royal Park* was eventually pulled off the Pier at 6.30 that morning. She had sustained limited damage and was taken into Cardiff for repair.

The Pier was insured for only £5,000 and it was obvious that a claim would have to be made against the owners of the ship. The *Penarth Times* for 22 May duly reported a writ had been issued. Repairing the damage was obviously going to be a long and complex job.

By early June the Council was considering the possibility of constructing a bailey bridge across the damaged portions, in a similar fashion to the one used to cope with the fire damage of 1931.

It was estimated that such a bridge would cost £1,600 and a request was made to the Ministry of Supply. At the same time it was also approved for deckchair accommodation to be provided on the landward portion. This was as a direct result of public requests and, besides, the Council needed the money.

Repair work began quickly. By October, Wallace Evans and Partners had provided a report which came up with two suggestions — either reconstruct the entire Pier in reinforced concrete or repair it in materials similar to the ones already in use. The Pier and Esplanade Committee asked for costings for both schemes. In the end it was decided to underpin the old cast-iron columns but also to place several new reinforced concrete ones, a compromise solution which still took 18 months to complete at a cost in the region of £28,000.

During the repairs the Pier remained closed but, finally, in May 1949 the *Penarth Times* was able to carry the following advertisement

'Opening Whit Sunday 4th June

The Penarth Pier

Official Opening by Chairman of Council, 10.15 am.

First boat calling for Weston 10.40 am.

Opening for promenading and all general purposes

from Official Opening Onwards.'

It had been hoped to have the Pier open by Easter but there were inevitable delays. The great day itself was overcast and gloomy and there were fears that the occasion would be spoiled. However, 'Sunshine broke through as the first crowds surged upon the Pier . . . following its official re-opening by the Chairman of the Council, Mr Gareth Roberts JP. Until then dull and threatening skies had prevailed, though colour was provided by the animated throng which filled the pavement at the entrace; the strings of coloured pennants which fluttered in the strong breeze against the White Marina building and the arc of shops, and the gaily trimmed dais from which the speeches were made. (*Penarth Times*, 9 June 1949)

Councillor Roberts cut the tape across the turnstile and formally announced the Pier once more open. The paddler *Glen Usk* — always a favourite with Penarth people — was already lying against the landing stage, pennants flying, and soon her decks were crowded with eager trippers. The Pier was back in business.

By the early 1950s Campbells were still operating six paddlers and one turbine steamer. However, they were finding it increasingly difficult to make ends meet. Motor cars were eating into their trade and public tastes were beginning to change once more. The increased mobility of holiday-makers either by car, 'bus or train, meant that several places could now be visited in one day. The appeal of spending the whole time on the same beach or pier, even the same paddle steamer, had long begun to pall.

Harsh economic decisions had to be made. The *Ravenswood* went to the breaker's yard in 1954, *Britannia* came out of service in 1956 and the *Glen Gower* a year later. Yet, despite this, Campbells maintained a regular service up and down the Channel, with Penarth Pier always featuring as a major calling point. The new paddlers *Bristol Queen* and *Cardiff Queen* soon became firm favourites with the Penarth public.

The minutes for the Pier and Esplanade Committee for 11 January 1954 fixed the charges for the season as follows:

'Entrance to Pier   2d per person
Hire of Deckchairs   3d per person (per 3 hours)
                            6d per day'.

At that stage bathing was still popular in the muddy waters of the Channel and the advent of a new phenomenon — Miners' Fortnight — gave Penarth something of an Indian Summer in terms of resort status. The coalmines had been nationalized in 1947 and, for the first time, miners — and associated tradesmen — were provided with genuine holidays with pay. An agreement between mine owners and unions had been reached in 1938, regarding paid holidays, but as deductive penalty fines were usually imposed whenever there was an absence from work, this had had only limited effect.

After the war, however, Miners' Fortnight — traditionally the last week in July and first in August — became a vital part of the South Wales holiday scene. The mines and most other industries closed down and resorts like Penarth enjoyed a new lease of life as whole families decamped to the seaside for their summer break. In 1958 Penarth boasted two hotels, four large guest houses and 75 boarding houses, mainly used to cater for these new holiday-makers.

With the Empire Games and the Festival of Wales being celebrated in the Principality that year, Campbell's paddlers, Penarth and its Pier saw plenty of activity. Like a candle which flares brightly and finally before it dies forever, the Welsh holiday scene was changing, however. The only trouble was — it did not realize it!

ABOVE: A cartoon from one of the local papers sums up the unique atmosphere of summer on Penarth Pier. (RG) BELOW: The *Port Royal Park* hit the Pier in 1947; it lies against the north side. The photograph was taken by Percy Stephens in the early morning of 3 May, before tugs dragged her free. (BS)

SPRING HAS COME! WHAT COULD BE MORE RELAXING THAN ANGLING BY THE SEASIDE? ONCE AGAIN THE POPULAR PENARTH

PIER MASTER, EX-C.P.O. S.GALLEY, D.S.M. TAKES HIS BEST UNIFORM OUT OF MOTHBALLS TO ADD DIGNITY TO THE PIER. ONE PENARTH

RESIDENT, MR MARK STOWERS, BELIEVES FISHING SHOULD BE DONE IN COMFORT.

SOME ENERGETIC SOULS FAVOUR LONG CASTS, UNDER THE IMPRESSION THAT THERE ARE MORE FISH AROUND THE FLAT HOLM THAN PENARTH PIER! WOMEN ARE BECOMING VERY KEEN ANGLERS.

MRS JAMES, WIFE OF A PENARTH DOCTOR SELDOM HAS TO PATRONIZE THE LOCAL FISHMONGERS.

ABOVE: Another Percy Stephens photograph shows the damage to the central portion of the Pier. BELOW: When the Pier re-opened in 1949 the *Glen Usk* was the first to call. (DA)

Penarth has always been well used by anglers. (HB) INSET: Stan Galley, Piermaster at Penarth between 1946 and 1970, is on the Pier in 1960. (RG)

This dramatic photograph shows the damage sustained when the *Bristol Queen* hit the Pier; Piermaster Stan Galley examines the consequences. (WM & E)

OLD FRIENDS FADE AWAY

The 1960s was an amazing decade which saw more social change than almost any of its predecessors. Penarth, like many other small communities, watched these changes and tried to adapt. As far as the Pier was concerned, it was a decade of great drama.

In June 1960 thousands of holiday-makers watched in horror from the Pier as a 425-ton dredger called *Ron Woolaway* suddenly capsized before their eyes. The channel into Cardiff Docks had to be constantly dredged to prevent it silting up and the clang of iron buckets had become almost second nature to the people of Cardiff and Penarth. Dozens of small boats from Penarth Beach plied around the up-ended dredger and the crew of seven escaped without injury.

This was not the first shipping accident off Penarth. In June 1958 the tug *Lavernock* had been in collision with the SS *Hurunui*, an 11,276 ton cargo vessel. The tug eventually sank in Cardiff Bay and one man lost his life. It was also not the last. The oil tanker *Regent Royal* ran aground on Penarth Head on 29 January 1965 and then, almost exactly 12 months later, the tug *Iselgarth* sank just 200 yards off the Pier. Having hit the propeller of the ship she was towing, the *Iselgarth* settled on the bottom with her funnel protruding from the water. Three men were missing after the accident.

In the great freeze of January 1963 the sea actually turned to ice. Small floes were to be seen on Penarth Beach, lying grouped around the Pier — a far cry from the hot summers which people normally associated with the town.

Some light entertainment was provided on the Pier — or, rather, below it — in August 1966. One of the acts booked for Penarth Holiday Week, escapologist Paul Denver, was suspended upside down from the Pier, clad in a straitjacket, and duly managed to get free. Hundreds of incredulous holiday-makers watched from the Esplanade and from below the Pier.

A moment of major drama came on 20 August 1966 when the Pier was involved in its second serious accident within 20 years. This time the guilty vessel was the White Funnel paddler *Bristol Queen*.

On that morning a thick fog lay across Penarth Head and a crowd of about 50 trippers had gathered at the end of the Pier, waiting for the scheduled 9.10 am sailing to Ilfracombe. The vessel was approximatley 15 minutes late and the would-be passengers were shivering with cold in the icy mist. Then, at last, the regular beat of paddle wheels was heard through the gloom. The *Bristol Queen* was coming. One eye-witness later said 'The fog was very thick but the klaxon on the pier was very faint — it wasn't any better than a car horn. We couldn't see the boat until it was within 20 yards'.

The sudden appearance of the paddler was startling. It was quickly apparent that she was too close and going too fast. The pier klaxon was sounded but the paddler paid no notice. Piermaster Stan Galley said 'She came in bows first, seemed to pull away and on the second attempt hit the pier and then came round broadside on'.

Another spectator confirmed this, stating that the paddler had appeared to shut off her engines just prior to hitting the Pier. The wind and tide, he felt, brought her into the woodwork.

Malcolm Davies, now Editor of the *Penarth Times*, was then a reporter on the paper. He remembers Councillor Glyn Salmon, Chairman of the Pier and Esplanade Committee, ringing him up to tell him that the *Bristol Queen* had hit the Pier. He offered to take Malcolm Davies there.

When they reached the sea-front, Council and pier officials were preventing spectators passing the entrance. Councillor Salmon brushed them aside and swept imperiously through. Malcolm Davies trailed after him. It was still foggy but, as they walked, they passed mangled railings and splintered timber. Then, suddenly, there was a gap in the fog. There, in front of them, so close they could almost touch it, was the huge iron bulk of a ship. More important, it was not moored or static but was heading directly towards them. Malcolm Davies remembers thinking 'God, we're dead!'. Both men took to their heels and ran for the Esplanade. Glyn Salmon, a dapper little man who always wore a bowler and carried a rolled umbrella, tore off up the Pier, his bowler bounding away seaward. To this day Malcolm Davies cannot remember who reached safety first.

The paddler was alongside for about 45 minutes before tugs managed to drag her free, the outgoing tide forcing her back and forth against the side of the Pier. It was this repeated banging which caused most of the damage — in addition to the spoiling of the ornate pier railings as the tugs dragged her free. Power lines to the shops and other services were also severed.

The *Bristol Queen* had hit the side of the Pier, not the landing stage, so steamer trips were not seriously affected. The Pier was closed briefly but re-opened later that day. The seward end remained closed to the public, for safety reasons, but a firework display planned for that evening went ahead. The *Bristol Queen* broke some plating and two portholes but was not long detained from her duties. Another Campbells' ship, *Westward Ho,* had appeared soon after the collision and many of the waiting passengers went on board her for an alternative trip to Minehead.

It was estimated that repairs would cost between £2,000 and £5,000 and these were carried out during the next few months. The following year a strong rumour began to circulate that the Council intended to sell the Pier to an entertainment promoter from the north. Nothing came of this proposal even though the toll profits were dropping and the Council seemed to be constantly having to find money for repairs, maintenance and regular upkeep.

The general shape of the sea-front was also changing. Balcony Villa and Rock Villa, built before 1880 and standing just to the south of the pier entrance, were demolished in 1963. A large, incongruous block of flats was built on the site. Many people felt that the character of the front was destroyed. The Pavilion, when it had been erected in 1929, had been greeted with horror but this was the last straw.

In 1959 the firm of P. & A. Campbell had come under the control of George Nott Industries — in reality, part of the Townsend Ferry Company. The early 1960s saw the introduction of motor vessels into the Channel, leaving only the two *Queens* to continue the paddler tradition. They continued to call at Penarth Pier and it became a favourite location, not just to board or leave the last paddlers, but to watch them beat elegantly away down-Channel.

St Trillo was the first of the new breed of motor vessels, closely followed by the *Vecta* which was renamed *Westward Ho* and served until 1971. For most of the 1960s Campbells fought a dogged battle for survival. It was always one-sided. The *Cardiff Queen* was withdrawn from service in 1966 and scrapped two years later. The *Bristol Queen* suffered the same indignity when she was towed away to Belgium for scrapping in March 1968, having damaged a paddle wheel off Barry. Given the long service of so many predecessors, the short lifespan of the *Bristol* and *Cardiff Queens* was tragic. Above all, it sums up the rapid decline of pleasure steamers in that era, not just in the Bristol Channel but around the whole of the British coast.

The paddlers might have gone but Campbells battled on, retiring *St Trillo* in 1969 but acquiring *Balmoral* the same year. The *Balmoral* was 'the last regular passenger ship to fly Campbells' house-flag. Under White Funnel management from 1969 to 1980 she was a widely travelled ship.' (*Passenger Steamers of the Bristol Channel*).

Penarth Pier suffered decline alongside the paddlers. Yet, hundreds of day-trippers came each summer and a large number still spent their time on the wooden decking, but the day of Penarth as a holiday resort was largely over. Foreign destinations were claiming more and more holiday traffic and Penarth now survived mainly as a day-trip centre. Yet the Pier had become more than just a structure. It had become a symbol for the town. As long as the Pier remained, many thought, Penarth would survive.

ABOVE: Penarth Pier in the evening sunlight. (HE) CENTRE: The *Bristol Queen* a▮
at Penarth Pier on Whit Sunday, 6 June 1965. The following year the paddler hit it
BELOW: The *Bristol Queen* is at anchor off Penarth on the evening of Sunday 20 June
Returning from Ilfracombe she developed paddle trouble as she arrived and was att▮
by two tugs. She later made her own way into Cardiff Docks. (CC)

E: The Pier, complete with Piermaster, c1970; the incongruous modern block of 1963 replaced the elegant Victorian buildings of the Esplanade. (RFC) BELOW: it which now stands on the end of the Pier is a far cry from the old Bijou Pavilion. (HB)

ABOVE: The Esplanade Hotel was destroyed by fire in 1977. For several years it remained, partly demolished, an eyesore to visitors and residents alike. (HB) BELOW: The Esplanade Hotel was eventually demolished in the late 1980s and a new block of flats erected (HB)

94

BACK TO THE BEGINNING

In 1970 Stan Galley retired as Piermaster. He had been employed for 24 years and, before that, had spent 25 in the Royal Navy. Finishing as a Chief Petty Officer, with the DSM to his credit, the Pier had become his life. During his service for the Council he had saved three lives and prevented the loss of many more. He was succeeded by Tom Fearnley who had already spent 10 years as leading hand on the Pier. Tom Fearnley was destined to be Penarth's last Piermaster but, at the time of his appointment, that was something nobody — least of all Mr Fearnley — even considered.

October 1970 saw yet another dramatic moment when two local men, Derek Wynne Jones and John Wilce, dived from the Pier to try to save an elderly woman. The water was twelve feet deep but both men hit the bottom when they jumped in. The woman, a confused and irrational 91-year-old, was unfortunately dead when pulled out.

The future of the Pier was in some doubt in 1970 as the reduction of pleasure steamer traffic and a falling away in the number of holiday-makers brought major problems. The *Penarth Times* for 5 June reported that the direct cost to the Council of keeping it open was only about £200 a year as fees from Campbells and entry tolls covered most of the expense. That year 6,723 passengers embarked on steamers from the Pier, the same figure as the previous year, even though the number of boats had been reduced from four to two. The number of calls made at the Pier had also been reduced from 470 to 446. All in all, it was felt to be worth keeping the place open but, even so, the Finance Committee, meeting later in the year, decided to ask Campbells for another £150 in fees to cover the shortfall.

Local Government re-organization in 1974 meant that the Pier underwent a change of ownership. Since 1924 it had belonged to the Penarth Urban District Council. Now it came under the remit of the new Vale of Glamorgan Borough Council, which was born on April Fools' Day 1974. The *Penarth Times* for 26 April reported that 'the Vale Council will control the Pier, Esplanade, Foreshore and shops associated with the Pier, the baths, the main parks and playing fields, the miniature golf course, bus shelters and public conveniences'.

The Town Council had hoped to retain control of many of the amenities, in particular the swimming baths. The Pier had lost much of its appeal and now the Baths had become more highly prized.

Three years later the sea-front lost another of its well-known attractions when the Esplanade Hotel caught fire and was burned down on Sunday 29 May 1977. It had traded since 1887, famous as the first home of the Barbarians Rugby Club. For many years the derelict and gutted building stood as a scar on the sea-front, before being finally demolished in the late 1980s.

The summer of 1979 was a poor one for Campbells. A new venture, White Funnel Steamers Ltd, was created in 1980 but this concentrated mainly on running supplies and trippers to Lundy Island. The following year there were no pleasure steamers in the Channel. Campbells' long history had come to an end and Penarth Pier stood forlorn, without purpose, for most of that summer.

The *South Wales Echo* for Thursday 7 July 1983 reported that the Vale Council was considering suggestions that the Pier should be sold. Running costs for 1982 had been £55,000. For 1983 they were expected to top £54,000. Despite these figures, the Pier was considered a vital part of the town and sale was rejected.

A little known collision occurred in May 1984 when the 35-foot ketch *Thelme* was swept into Penarth Pier after her engine had failed. She had been making for her moorings in Cardiff Docks when the problem occurred. Piermaster Thomas Fearnley quickly lowered a rope ladder and two of the crew were able to use it to escape. The owners of the yacht were rescued by the Penarth Inshore Lifeboat. Tom Fearnley had called for assistance and the tug *Uskgarth* attempted to tow the yacht away. However, the *Thelme* went down before the tow line could be secured.

The yacht did no damage to the structure of the Pier but her mast had fouled the roof of the toilet block. In the end the yacht sank alongside and was able to be inspected and, indeed, walked around at low water.

Tom Fearnley, Penarth's last Piermaster, retired in May 1985. The *Western Mail* commemorated his departure in an article about the Pier, commenting that 'A quarter of a century ago ... the Piermaster was not just the Piermaster but he was a one-man tourist information centre. He would spend his day attending to the arrival of passenger boats at the end of the pier. There would be six or seven people employed on the pier to look after the boat, the deck chairs and the pier office'.

How times change! Prior to Tom Fearnley's departure another important change had taken place when tolls were abolished. This decision was taken at a Committee Meeting of the Vale Council on 16 October 1984 and came into operation on 1 April 1985. The Pier was no longer to provide an income but had become an amenity, paid for out of the rates. For several years the Pier became merely a quaint tourist attraction. The Marina — which had changed its name to the Commodore — continued to be a centre for dances and, later, functioned as a snooker club. An arcade, with fruit machines and video games, was also added. There were still shops and a Vale Tourist Information Centre. Yet, in the early '80s the Pier seemed somewhat stranded, a structure without a purpose. Quite simply, it needed pleasure steamers.

However, the Paddle Steamer Preservation Society, founded in 1959 by a group of paddle steamer enthusiasts, had definite plans for the Pier. The *Bristol Queen* and *Cardiff Queen* may have been scrapped somewhat prematurely but when, in 1974, the Clyde paddler *Waverley* was offered to the Society, the Scottish members knew that it was too good a chance to miss. They eagerly accepted. For several years the re-vamped *Waverley* cruised on the Clyde and even made two weekend visits to the Bristol Channel in the last days of the White Funnel Fleet.

Since then, she has visited the area every year, gradually increasing the length of her stays as the popularity of the trips grew. It is one of life's great ironies that, within ten years of the final demise of Campbells' White Funnel Fleet, enthusiasm for Bristol Channel cruising was rejuvenated to such an extent that people could not get enough of the old *Waverley*. In 1986 she was supplemented by the *Balmoral* which had also been acquired by the Paddle Steamer Preservation Society.

Penarth Pier has now become the central point for Bristol Channel cruises by both the *Waverley* and the *Balmoral* — this, despite the fact that it has become considerably more tidal than at previous stages of its history. It is now estimated that over 30,000 people tramp across the planks of the Pier every year, just to embark on the cruise ships. It is possible that an equal number annually use it to walk on or fish from, thus giving a total number of around 60,000 visitors every year. If that figure is anything like accurate, it means that Penarth Pier is as well used now as it ever was in its glorious past.

HM Coastguard, like the lifeboat service, had maintained a regular presence on Penarth seafront for many years. For a long while the Coastguard used the Pier as an actual base. However, a new sector base was created on Cliff Parade and when this opened in July 1987 the Coastguard left the Pier. From this new HQ the Coastguard maintains a close watch on their sector, an area which stretches from Aberthaw in the west to Gloucester in the east.

The popularity of the Pier was as great as ever in the 1990s. Thanks to the Paddle Steamer Preservation Society it had regained

a new lease of life. It was with some disquiet, therefore, that t
Penarth Times of 3 September 1993 announced 'Doubt over t
future of Penarth Pier. The long term future of Penarth Pier h
been thrown into doubt by the need to spend up to £500,000 c
repairs'.

As a Grade II listed building and as a major tourist attractio
the possibility of losing the Pier caused an outcry in Penart
Demolition, however, was not really viable, unless repair costs we
astronomical. By giving a range of options — from total repair
one end of the spectrum to demolition at the other — the Va
Council was merely mapping out the possibilities it had in min
Yet fear of the Pier being smashed down did not easily go away

If the structure needed such major repairs, people said, then
was a price which must be paid. After all, what would Penarth I
without its Pier? Clearly work needed to be carried out — time ar
the elements had caused major problems — but demolition shou
not be countenanced.

A decision was soon made to undertake a detailed survey in ord
to find out exactly what work needed to be done. £100,000 w
put asside by the Council. At the same time, with the Pier fina
in its centenary year, money was earmarked for celebrating.

At the time of writing the results of the survey are still awaite
but there is every reason to look to the future with hope ar
certainty. Money has been set aside and there is every likelihoc
that repairs — major, minor or somewhere in between — will t
carried out. That is as it should be. The people of Penarth, tl
Paddle Steamer Preservation Society and trippers to the town a
need it to survive. Its history is a fine one — its future should t
even finer.

Penarth Pier in 1993; one of the highest tides for several years nearly swamped the d
(HB)

EPILOGUE

Pleasure piers were a unique phenomenon which, somehow, seem to sum up the Victorian seaside resort. So many of them have now disappeared, leaving only rare photographs and postcards to mark their passing. Many of them encountered difficulties similar to those which afflicted Penarth Pier — being hit by ships and catching fire were just two of the major occupational hazards. Storms also caused difficulties.

The briefest of surveys into the damage sustained by piers will show how vulnerable they were to the elements. Aberystwyth Pier, for example, opened on Good Friday 1865 but in January over a hundred feet were washed away in a storm. Fire severely damaged Morecambe West End, Ramsgate, Paignton and Shanklin piers. Colwyn Bay Pier was actually burned twice — in 1922 and again in 1933.

So for Penarth Pier to survive all that the elements and fate's fickle finger threw at it, is nothing short of amazing. It remains as a tribute to long gone times, to a quieter, more sedate age with simpler pleasures and a sense of both place and purpose. Like the paddle steamers it was originally built to serve, it evokes strong feelings of nostalgia.

And yet it is also a fully functional structure, one which is as well used now as it was a hundred years ago. 1994 marks the Pier's centenary. Hopefully it will be there, on the seafront of Penarth, in another hundred years' time. If this book can commemorate the past but also look to the future with both hope and belief then it will have fulfilled its purpose. Quite simply, read the book, then go and stand on the Pier. Enjoy getting in touch with part of your heritage — that is the only real way of making sure Penarth Pier survives for another century.

BIBLIOGRAPHY

Adamson, Simon *Seaside Piers*, Batsford 1977

Anon *The White Funnel Fleet Handbook*, P & A Campbell undated

Anon *Penarth: Official Guide*, undated

Benjamin, E. Alwyn *Penarth, 1841-71*, Brown & Sons 1980

Bevan, Ernest T *Old Penarth*, unpublished MS 1949

Carradice, Phil & Best, George *Beside the Seaside: South Wales in Camera*, Quotes Ltd 1992

Coombes, Nigel *Passenger Steamers of the Bristol Channel*, Twelveheads Press 1990

Egan, David *Coal Society*, Gomer 1987

Francis, Hywel & Smith, Dai *The Fed*, Laurence & Wishart 1980

Gibbs, John Morel *Morels of Cardiff: the History of a Family Shipping Firm*, National Museum of Wales 1982

Hilling, J.B *The Buildings of Llandaff, Penarth and Outer Cardiff: a Historical Survey*, article in *Glamorgan Historian Vol 17*

Ings, David *Penarth in Old Picture Postcards*, Vol 1 & 2, European Library 1985 & 1990

Mead, Diana *Development of Penarth as a Seaside Resort*, unpublished MS 1984

Phillips, A. K. *Development of Penarth*, article in South Wales Institute of Architects *Journal* Vol 3, No 3 September 1959

Thorne, Roy *Penarth: A History*, Starling Press Vol 1 & 2 1976

Tilney, Chrystal *A History of Penarth with Lavernock*, privately printed 1988

Williams, C. W. *Mate's Illustrated Penarth*, Penarth Urban District Council 1903

Newspapers

Most of the research for this book was carried out through use of the excellent local newspapers of the town and region, particularly for the period 1888-1966. These are held in Penarth Library and Cardiff Central Library: *The Penarth Times, The Penarth News, The Penarth Observer, The Western Mail, The South Wales Echo.*

Original Documents

Penarth Promenade & Pier Order, 1892

Penarth Pier and Harbour Act, 1924

Minutes of Penarth Urban District Council & Pier Esplanade Committee, 1939-1954.

Accounts of Penarth Urban District Council *re* Penarth Pier, 1924-1930

SUBSCRIBERS

Presentation copies

1 Vale of Glamorgan Borough Council
2 Penarth Town Council
3 Penarth Library
4 Glamorgan Record Office
5 Paddle Steamers Preservation Society

6 Phil & Trudy Carradice
7 Clive & Carolyn Birch
8 David Howell-Jones
9 Colin & Karen Parker
10- Phil Carradice
11
12- Charles & Freda
13 Carradice
14 Mary Carradice
15- Nancy Jones
18
19 John Hiley
20 Patricia Ann Mather
21 Jill Slade
22 Irene Atherton
23 B. Davies
24 W.H. Cuss
25 Ivan James
26 Deborah Haswell
27 Miss J. Nye
28 Mrs D. Lewis
29 Mike Evans
30 John Derham
31 Adrian Gray
32 W. Vanstone
33 Nigel Fearnley
34 Hazel Fearnley
35 Glynne Thomas
36 Mike Joseph
37 Mr & Mrs H. J. Speake
38 P.J. Collins
39- Miss M. Dunkley
40
41 Colin Brinkworth
42 Les Fearn
43 Phil Stockwell
44 Brian & Barbara
   Brooke
45 Graham Illingworth
46 Dave Floyd
47 Mary Bishop
48 Ian Dewar
49 Pembrokeshire
   County Library
50 HM Coastguard
51 R.J. Ridout
52 R.D. Llewellyn
53 Mrs Phyllis Jones
54 Audrey Diamond
55 Brian T. Stephens
56 Michael C. Stephens

57 Pamela M. Page
58 Mrs Mary L. Morris
59 Dave & Linda Randel
60 Hugh Bousie
61 Ron Bousie
62 Margaret Andrews
63 Penarth Local History
   Society
64 Jean Beer
65 Jill & Mick Spiller
66 David Smith
67 Mrs Florence Parry
68 Judith Lanning
69 George & Enid Best
70 Ivan Sharpe
71 Don & Sue Murray
72 Ray Coombes
73 Margaret & David
   Allen-Oliver
74 A.R. Thorne
75 Edwin Thorne
76 Victoria Ringrose
77 Les Hall
78 P.A. Johnson
79 Florence Evans
80 Ruth & John Young
81 Lynne Hutchings
82 G.J. Rideout
83 S.J. Rideout
84 Robert Galley
85- J.H. Lawrence
87
88 Mr Harris
89 Marian Johns
90 Jean Davies
91 P.M. Davies
92 Glyn Johnson
93 Anne Hughes
94 Frances & Philip Harris
95 Doug Pattison
96 Judith & Lennie
   Scourfield
97- Headlands School
111
112 Phil Spillane
113 Mr & Mrs W.D.
   Barberini
114 Mrs E. Lewis
115- South Glamorgan
122 County Libraries
123 Dr Jonathan Jones

124 Mrs Mary L Morris
125 Cecilia M. Rawnson
126 Sandra & Geoffrey
   Leat
127 Margaret Butler,
   Wales official tourist
   guide
128 Mair McColl,
   St Margarets
   Residential Home
129 Edward J. Vick
130 Loretta & Nigel Gibbs
131 John Mahoney
132 Glynne Holmes
133 Robin Thomas Croydon
134 J.A. Gatheridge
135 Mrs J.M. Young
136 Mike Smith
137 Dr Nigel J. Morgan
138 Linda Green
139 Gladys Thomson
140 Douglas Rex Wilson
141 Colin Churchill
142 Arthur R. Payne
143 Richard A. Davies
144 Pauline Thomas
145 Terry Buckingham
146 Ann Mules
147 Jane Chick
148 Sally & Terry Hart
149 Michael Dugmore
150 Robert L. Eastleigh
151 Raymond Jones
152 Edwin James Evans
153 Claire Louise Price
154 Lt Col (ret'd)
   G.C. Hall TD
155 Mrs J.L. Churchll
156 Peter Stealey
157 D.R. & T. Franklin
158 Paul Brinkworth
159 The Penarth Society
160 Mrs Audrey Poole
161 James R.M. Ernest
162 Cllr Anthony Ernest
163 Andrew Rabaiotti
164 Iris Jones
165 Terry Sylvester
166 Nick Koops
167 South Glamorgan
   Libraries

168 Gwyneth White	198 Steven Gimber	226 Shelley Enticott
169 Stan M. Rees	199 Rosalie Gimber	227 Stanley W.G. Preece
170 Barbara Brown	200 L.S. Thomas	228 Martin Nelson
171 Andrew Johnson	201 Geoff & Sue Warren	229 Sidney Robinson
172 A.J. Brown	202 Sqn Ldr K.E. Shell	230 Kenneth F. Floyd
173 Myra & John Allen	RAF (retd)	231 Alan Wakeman
174 Pat & Colwyn Wiliams	203 Tony Williams	232 Norman Bird
175 John Carter	204 Mr & Mrs T.G.	233 Bernard See
176 Jeremy Carter	Simmons	234 J.H. Fraser
177 W. Haydn Burgess	205 H.J. Vincent	235 Michael Carden
178 J.M. Gold	206 L. Gordon Reed	236 R.E. Connett
179 Iaian Dewar	207 Stan & Joan Rendell	237 Jonathan Davies
180 Keith Thomas	208 M.A. Tedstone	238 O. J. Scott
181 Philip Dalling	209 Ian A. Aitken-Kemp	239 Victor Gray
182 John Samuel	210 Duncan Rees	240 Mr & Mrs R.D. Dixo
183 H.G. Spriggs	211 E.V. Ashworth	241 Alec K. Pope
184 M.R. Kelly	212 Barbara & Alan Evans	242 Dr J. D. Naysmith
185 Emma E. Spears	213 W.N.E. Ledbury	243 Dennis P. Nowell
186 Margaret I. Usher	214 Vaughan Roderick	244 Sherlyn Henly
187 David Vanner	215 Keith Clode	245 Michael Sullivan
188 Clive Seaton	216 G. Alfred Gough	246 John Piddocke
189 Clive & Kate Todd	217 George Thomas Dupe	247 Guy Piddocke
190 Clive P. Williams	218 Harold Whatley	248 Tom Shell
191-192 N.D.H.Q. Coombes	219 Eric Freeman	249 Daisy P. Fisher
	220 Christopher Henton	250 Robert Milford
193 P.J. Murrell	221 J. Donaldson	251 Eric H. Chamberlain
194 S.F. Wake	222 Dorothy Milner	252 J. W. Forster Brown
195 Michael Parsons	223 Kenneth Howell	253 Beresford Johnson
196 Ivy Moindrot	224 The Clinch Family	Allen
197 Stanley Say	225 B.V. Elward	254 Janet Munn
		(Remaining names unlisted)

A last view of the Pier, as it should be remembered, with the tide in and
a fully loaded paddle steamer ready to cruise away down-Channel. (HB)